WHAT TO COOK WHEN Everyone's HUNGRY

100 deliciously full-flavour
weeknight fixes

WHAT TO COOK WHEN *Everyone's* HUNGRY

Shelina Permalloo

EBURY
PRESS

06 Introduction

10 Get Yourself Organised

BREAKFASTS FOR BUSY MORNINGS

14

16 Loaded Breakfast Quiche
18 Coconut Mango Overnight Oats
20 Speedy Masala Beans
21 Creamy Corn Pudding
22 Roti Canai Eggs With a Mango Twist
24 Pistachio Croissants
26 Spicy Egg Bagel
27 Golden Air-fryer Muffins
28 Fluffy Yoghurt Pancakes
30 Chilla – Chickpea and Spinach Pancakes

LUNCHTIME HEROES

34

36 Chipotle Chicken Bowl
38 Fresh and Crunchy Summer Rolls
39 Sticky Mushroom Rice
40 Mango and Halloumi Shake-Up Salad
42 Crispy Rice Salad
44 Spicy Tuna and Cucumber Salad
45 Creamy Coconut Tomato Daal
46 Harissa Roasted Pumpkin and Chickpeas
48 Spicy Sweetcorn Fritters
50 Sushi Rice Waffle, Tomatoes and a Crispy Chilli Oil

ALL IN ONE POT

52

54 Green Biriyani
56 Salmon Teriyaki Rice
58 Creamy Garlic Chicken Pasta
60 Mauritian Moon Fan Braised Chicken Rice
62 Mauritian Noodles
64 Black Bean Stew with Plantain
65 Chicken Bulgur Pilaf
66 Lamb Meatball Red Thai Curry
68 Cajun Seafood Stew
70 Mauritian Roti Beef
71 Turkish Lamb and Aubergine Traybake
72 Chicken Jollof

WHIP IT UP IN 15

74

76 Prawns in Creole Sauce
78 Pineapple Fried Rice with Cashews
80 Tuna Suugo with Baasta
81 Paratha Chilli-Cheese Rolls
82 Turkish Pizza Bread
84 Cevapi – Juicy Grilled Balkan Kebabs
86 Rainbow Noodles
88 Corned Beef Rougaille
89 Smoky Chickpeas with Sundried Tomatoes
90 Chill Beef with Broccoli
92 Korean Tofu Jjigae
94 Savoury Cabbage Pancakes

COMFORTING CROWD-PLEASERS — 96

- 98 Pull-apart Pizza Rolls
- 100 Air-fried Chicken
- 102 Prawn and Plantain Curry
- 104 Moroccan Vegetable Tagine
- 106 Chicken Peri Peri Traybake
- 108 Prawn Butter Masala
- 110 Saturday Soup with Dumplings
- 112 Udon and Dumpling Ramen
- 114 Moroccan Harira
- 115 Mauritian Carrot and Red Lentil Soup
- 116 'Marry Me' Salmon
- 118 Blackened Salmon Tacos with Mango Salsa
- 120 Mauritian Moulouktani Chicken
- 121 Domoda – Peanut Stew with Okra and Sweet Potato
- 122 Air-fryer Kebabs
- 124 Five-ingredient Coconut Chicken Curry

EVERYDAY HEROES — 126

- 128 Spaghetti Bolognese
- 130 Nasi Goreng
- 132 Cheesy Microwave Mac Magic
- 134 Chicken Shawarma
- 136 Thai Coconut Curry Noodle Soup
- 138 Brown Stew Salmon
- 139 Satay Chicken Drumsticks
- 140 Turkish-style Pasta with Garlic Yoghurt
- 142 Chicken Traybake Kebabs
- 144 Five-Spice Beef Noodles
- 146 Miso Honey Aubergine Steaks
- 148 Chilli Beef Burritos with 'Cheese Wings'

EASY EXTRAS — 150

- 152 Veggie Rotis
- 154 Quick Cheesy Naan
- 156 Garlicky Lemon Broccoli
- 157 Pima Crazer – Mauritian Chilli Sauce
- 158 The Best Roast Potatoes
- 160 Honeyed Carrots
- 161 Plantains
- 162 Sweetcorn Ribs
- 164 Zasar Legim – Spicy Mauritian Pickled Vegetables
- 166 Everyday Rice
- 167 Golden Spiced Rice
- 167 Red Rice
- 168 Batata Harira

SWEET FIXES — 170

- 172 Miso Chocolate Cookies
- 174 Classic Mauritian Maspain
- 175 Cookie For Mama
- 176 Air-fryer Cherry Pie Pockets
- 178 Pistachio and Rose Loaf
- 180 White Chocolate and Raspberry Tiramisu
- 182 Mango Lime Lollies
- 183 Ghriba – Moroccan Cookies
- 184 Coconut Basbousa
- 186 Cinnamon Doughnuts
- 188 Crinkle Baklava Tray
- 190 Funfetti Traybake
- 192 Air-fryer S'mores
- 194 Swiss Roll Cake
- 196 Easy Pistachio Barfi
- 198 Microwave Shortbread
- 200 The Ultimate Chocolate Cake in 15 minutes!

- 204 Appliance Guide Throughout the Book
- 205 Ingredient Sharing: Don't Waste It
- 206 Shelina's 7 Day Meal Plan
- 208 Get to Know Your Spices
- 210 Batch-cooking Tips
- 212 Index
- 218 Conversion Guides
- 220 Acknowledgements

Introduction

What do you cook when everyone's hungry, time is short and energy is running low? It's a question I've faced countless times, and it's exactly why I wrote this book. I wanted to create something you can turn to when you need a reliable, no-fuss meal that still feels like proper home cooking. All the recipes on these pages fit into real life and are designed to take the stress out of midweek meals and help you to put something satisfying on the table without spending hours in the kitchen.

I've spent more than a decade working as a professional chef, but the most important part of my life's journey has been being a single mum to my seven-year-old daughter. On top of that, I'm the cook of the family, the one who feeds everyone: my child, my relatives, my friends, and whoever else happens to drop by! My home has always been a place where food is shared, and where no one ever leaves hungry. That's how I was raised in my Mauritian household, where we were taught to be resourceful, to waste nothing and to stretch what we had in order to feed as many as possible. But being a single mum, I had to take those lessons even further. I had to find ways to make cooking easier, faster and more manageable, while also keeping it delicious, flavourful and nourishing.

Like so many of you, I juggle multiple roles. I work full-time, I run my own businesses and I'm always on the go. But one thing I refuse to do is rely on ready meals or take-aways to feed myself or my child during the week – they're absolutely fine once in a while as a treat, but I truly believe that preparing good food doesn't have to be complicated. I want to share what I've learned over the years to show you how simple it can be to cook from scratch, even on your busiest days. These recipes have been tested in my own kitchen, in my real life, where there's no sous chef to chop my ingredients and no team of staff to clean up afterwards. Just me, myself and I, cooking meals that truly work, day after day, week after week; meals that are quick to prepare, with limited mess, and that genuinely make life easier.

Beyond the practical side of things, food has always been deeply personal to me. It's about love, culture and connection. My friendships span the world, and through them I've been able to experience different cuisines, ingredients and cooking styles. This book reflects all those influences; a mix of childhood nostalgia, family traditions and global flavours that have shaped the way I cook and eat at home. It's a celebration of food that's comforting, vibrant and full of life. I hope that when you open this book, you feel inspired. I want it to feel like a friend in the kitchen, guiding you towards meals that are doable, enjoyable and, most importantly, satisfying.

So, whether you're cooking for family, feeding yourself or making something to share with friends, I hope this book brings you some ease, some inspiration and a lot of good food. Let's make midweek cooking something to enjoy, rather than something to stress about.

Shelina

Get Yourself Organised!
CLEAR THE CLUTTER, CLEAR YOUR MIND

Before we dive into cooking, let's talk about something that will make your life so much easier, and that's getting your kitchen in order! Trust me, this book works best when you have a few key things sorted at home. If you're anything like me, you probably have crockery and cutlery that you adore but only use on 'special occasions'. And let's be honest, you also have pots and pans collecting dust, like that beautiful tagine that you bought on a trip to Morocco and swore you'd use . . . The ugly truth? You use it once, maybe twice, a year – and even then only decoratively! You should probably assess after six months, and if you haven't used certain items, you can sell them on Vinted or pop them up in the loft. The key is to get any superfluous kit out of your kitchen.

FREEZER PREP AND SAFE REHEATING

Prepping food for the freezer is a great way to save time and reduce waste; it makes busy weeknights easier knowing that some of the work is already done and waiting in the freezer! You can portion up batch-cooked recipes or leftovers into airtight containers, label them with the date and freeze for up to 3 months, then simply defrost and reheat fully when needed.

When it comes to staples like rice or pasta, you can prepare this ahead or store leftovers, but rice in particular does need special care, as it can harbour bacteria even after cooking. Always cool it quickly – usually within an hour of cooking – and do so at room temperature, not in the fridge (for speedy cooling, drain the just-cooked rice and hold the sieve under cold running water). Once cool, refrigerate or freeze in a sealed container immediately to avoid bacterial growth. When needed, reheat thoroughly until piping hot all the way through.

For all foods, avoid reheating more than once. For best results, defrost frozen meals in the fridge overnight or use a microwave's defrost setting before reheating, then heat until piping hot throughout.

THE ESSENTIALS: WHAT YOU ACTUALLY NEED

Knives and gadgets:

- ○ A standard chef's knife – 20cm is perfect. This should be your main knife, heavy enough for chopping onions, light enough for herbs. Keep it sharp and it'll never let you down.
- ○ Small paring knife for peeling, trimming and delicate jobs. Small but mighty.
- ○ Speed peeler for potatoes and hard vegetables.
- ○ Lime squeezer (Mexican elbow).
- ○ Microplane for grating garlic/ginger/Parmesan.
- ○ Kitchen scissors for snipping herbs, cutting meat and opening packaging – much easier than using a knife sometimes.
- ○ Digital scales, for accurate measuring.
- ○ Waffle iron – handy for rice waffles and breakfast waffles for kids, and small enough to tuck away in a cupboard when you're not using it.

A few storage essentials:

- ○ A couple of clip-and-seal containers.
- ○ Some Mason jars – a mix of larger and smaller, individual-sized ones.
- ○ Microwave-safe containers and bowls – I have a 25 x 10cm, 1-litre glass container that is ideal for cooking a range of microwave meals.
- ○ Small and large glass bowls for mixing and marinating.

Two baking trays:

- ○ A loaf tin for bread, banana loaves and beyond.
- ○ A rectangular tray for brownies, traybakes and other easy bakes.

(Let's be real, no one is baking tiered cakes on a Wednesday night. Pop those round cake tins under the stairs and thank me later.)

Three pots and pans:

- ○ A deep, 30cm saucepan with a lid for stews, curries, soups and all those one-pot wonders.
- ○ A medium saucepan for boiling pasta, cooking veggies or making smaller meals.
- ○ A standard frying pan for eggs, roti or for a quick sauté of veggies, meat or fish.

(I confess – I also have a tiny egg pan for my daughter, who is obsessed with eggs. It also works for small pancake batches, but you only really need the three pans mentioned above.)

And that's it. The rest? You don't need it. The more clutter in your kitchen, the harder it is to get through midweek meals without stress. Decluttering isn't just about tidying up; it's about making your life easier, calmer and more enjoyable so you can reach for what you need without rummaging high and low for those everyday pots, pans and trays.

LET'S TALK ABOUT FLAVOUR HEROES

Now that your kitchen's all set, let's talk about flavour heroes. You don't need a whole rack containing every ingredient under the sun; just a handful of essentials will make all the difference. The secret? Get yourself a spice shelf and set it close to the stove, so you can easily reach for what you need when cooking. Trust me, it'll save you time and stress. To make life easier, I like to cluster my heroes into three main categories: Sauces, Spices and Can't Live Without. Here's how I organise them.

Sauces

These are the ones I use for quick flavour hits:

- ○ Soy sauce
- ○ Oyster sauce
- ○ Browning
- ○ Chilli sauces
- ○ Harissa paste
- ○ Ketjap manis
- ○ Turkish tomato paste
- ○ Garlic and ginger paste

Spices

These are my go-to flavour bombs that make every dish pop:

- ○ Curry powder (mild or hotter depending on your heat preference)
- ○ Ground cumin
- ○ Ground coriander
- ○ Ground turmeric
- ○ Garam masala
- ○ Ground allspice
- ○ Ground cinnamon

Can't live without

These are my everyday staples that I always reach for:

- ○ Garlic powder
- ○ Paprika
- ○ Dried mixed herbs
- ○ Vegetable boullion powder (this adds extra flavour and umami in lots of dishes)
- ○ Stock cubes
- ○ Salt
- ○ Ground black pepper

Group them together so you know exactly where to go when you need them. The key is to make sure they're easily accessible, so you don't waste any time hunting for the right jar or bottle.

A little organisation goes a long way and will help streamline your cooking process. Once everything is where it needs to be, midweek meals will feel like a breeze!

BREAKFASTS FOR *Busy Mornings*

Mornings can be the busiest part of the day, when time is tight, patience is thin and the to-do list is already a mile long! These breakfast recipes are so simple – and they're also speedy, with each one taking no more than 20 minutes to prepare. So, whether you're rushing to get out the door or just need a stress-free start to your day, these breakfasts will help you get through your morning in record time, with no fuss and no hassle but all the flavour you need to feel full and happy. Quick, delicious and satisfying, these recipes are the perfect way to fuel your day when you need it most.

SERVES: 2-4　　　　　　　　　　　　　　　　　PREP + COOK TIME: 15 minutes

LOADED BREAKFAST QUICHE

These quiche slices are perfect for breakfast, especially on those days when you know lunch will be late or you have a heavy workload ahead of you. The quiche is packed with veggies, and is ideal for using up whatever you have lying around. This is a versatile recipe and certainly not one for purists!

1. Lay the tortilla in a round, flat-bottomed, ovenproof bowl, gently pressing down to form a raised edge all the way around the bowl.
2. Crack the eggs directly into the tortilla. Add the peas, sweetcorn, Cajun seasoning and half of the grated Cheddar. Whisk everything together.
3. Sprinkle the remaining cheese on top and arrange the tomato halves over the mixture.
4. Air-fry at 160°C for 10 minutes, until the quiche is set and slightly golden.
5. Cut into slices and serve warm.

25cm tortilla (gluten-free if needed)

3 medium eggs

2 tbsp frozen peas

2 tbsp frozen sweetcorn

1 tbsp Cajun seasoning

50g medium Cheddar, grated

6 baby plum tomatoes, halved

SERVES: 2

PREP + COOK TIME: 5 minutes

COCONUT MANGO OVERNIGHT OATS

I find overnight oats so helpful when I have early-morning meetings and need my life sorted from the moment I wake up. They are easy to prepare ahead and take on the go, and are especially useful for car journeys. My brother laughs at me because my car is an extension of my home, and I let my daughter eat in it when we are rushing around. Once a year, my brother has the pleasure of removing my daughter's car seat and doing a deep clean for me – he calls that part of the car 'rocky road' because of all the crumbs and bits of food! Whatever your car habits, make these oats and travel with them, because, honestly, they will save your mornings.

1. In a bowl, mix the coconut milk with the oats, cinnamon and maple syrup, then divide between 2 small Mason jars or lidded containers. Top with the mango chunks and cover with the lid. Leave in the fridge overnight.

2. When ready to serve, top with flaked almonds and a few extra chunks of mango.

400ml tin of full-fat coconut milk

125g rolled oats (use gluten-free oats if needed; I like the Glebe Farm brand)

1 tsp ground cinnamon

1 tbsp maple syrup (or honey if non-vegan)

1 large mango, peeled and chopped into small chunks

TOPPINGS

Handful of flaked almonds

Dollop of coconut yoghurt

SERVES: 2   PREP + COOK TIME: 5 minutes

SPEEDY MASALA BEANS

Masala beans have been part of my repertoire since I was introduced to them by the Uppal family – my friends who became family while I was at university. I never knew that the frugal and cheap tin of beans could be transformed in such a beautiful way. Once I had my daughter, I had to find shortcuts for making breakfast before school, so I've made this microwave-friendly – and, of course, time-friendly. It's perfect for mornings when you need that extra pick-me-up. Packed with protein and fibre, beans are a great way to start your day as they keep you full.

415g tin of baked beans
1 tsp garam masala
¼ tsp ground turmeric
¼ tsp Kashmiri chilli powder
1 tsp garlic and ginger paste
1 tbsp tomato ketchup
½ tsp cumin seeds

SERVE (OPTIONAL)
2 slices of sourdough
Dollop of Greek-style yoghurt
1 tbsp chopped coriander
¼ red onion, finely chopped

1. Place the beans and all the flavourings into a microwave-safe container and cook on High for 1 minute. Stir the ingredients thoroughly, then cook for a further 30 seconds until piping hot all the way through.

2. In the meantime, toast some sourdough, if you like, then pour the spicy masala beans over the toast. Top with a dollop of yoghurt, then sprinkle over some coriander and red onion, and serve.

SERVES: 6 **PREP + COOK TIME: 15 minutes**

CREAMY CORN PUDDING

Growing up in a Mauritian family, this was our morning staple, usually made with coconut and raisins. I like to add some fresh fruit on top but keep the island flavours of vanilla and coconut running through. It took my daughter some time to develop a love for this dish, but there's something about it that immediately transports me back to being in my mum's kitchen as a child.

1. In a medium saucepan, combine the cornmeal, coconut milk, sugar and cardamom pods and bring to a boil. The mixture will start to thicken after 3–4 minutes of cooking. At this point, add the raisins, coconut, vanilla and salt, and reduce the heat to low-medium. Continue to cook for a few minutes, adding extra coconut milk if you prefer a thinner texture. You do need to keep stirring, as cornmeal can quickly catch and burn at the bottom of the pan.

2. To check if the cornmeal is cooked, place a small bit of the mixture between your fingers and rub together. If it feels like sand, it needs more cooking; give it a further 3–4 minutes. If it dissolves with some pressure, it's ready. Check the consistency of the whole pudding, too, and add more coconut milk, if needed, depending on your taste. Discard the cardamom shells before serving.

3. You can eat this just as it is, or top it with passion fruit, mango and toasted coconut flakes for a tropical feel.

75g coarse cornmeal

500ml full-fat coconut milk (from a carton), plus extra if needed

75g golden caster sugar

2 cardamom pods, smashed open

75g raisins

25g desiccated coconut

½ tsp vanilla extract, or a pinch of vanilla powder

¼ tsp salt

TOPPINGS (OPTIONAL)

Chopped passion fruit

Chopped mango

Toasted coconut flakes

SERVES: 2   PREP + COOK TIME: 10 minutes

ROTI CANAI EGGS WITH A MANGO TWIST

I first found frozen roti canai at my local international shop, and took the pleasure of bulk-buying and packing them into my chest freezer. But when I saw them in my mainstream supermarket freezer aisle, I knew that I wasn't the only one with a secret! Frozen roti, roti canai, naan, paratha, chapati – all of these are a MUST. If you find them, buy them. I promise you one thing: no one will know. This breakfast is the perfect pick-me-up for cold starts to the day or when you need some flavour to get you moving. A little heat, a lot of comfort, and a whole load of fast flavour!

2 medium eggs
¼ tsp curry powder
¼ tsp ground cumin
salt, to taste
2 frozen roti canai
1 tsp oil
1 tomato, finely chopped
¼ red onion, sliced into half-moons

GARNISH
2 tbsp mango chutney
roughly chopped coriander
1 mini cucumber, sliced

1. In a bowl, whisk the eggs with curry powder, cumin and salt until smooth and slightly frothy.

2. Heat a frying pan over a medium heat. Add one of the frozen roti canai and cook quickly, around 3 minutes, on both sides, until it begins to colour. Remove from the pan and repeat with the second roti canai, then set aside.

3. Add half of the oil to the frying pan followed by half the tomato and onions. Sauté for a few minutes, then pour in half of the egg mixture.

4. Let the omelette cook for 1–2 minutes until the edges begin to set but the centre is still runny.

5. Cover the omelette with one of the roti canai and cook for another minute.

6. Flip the omelette and cook for another 2–3 minutes until the base of the roti canai is crispy. Set aside to keep warm and repeat with the remaining ingredients to make a second roti canai omelette.

7. Top the omelettes with mango chutney, coriander and chopped cucumber. Wrap them up and enjoy!

SERVES: 4 PREP + COOK TIME: 10 minutes

PISTACHIO CROISSANTS

A great way to use up day-old croissants – imagine an almond croissant but infinitely better, stuffed with a pistachio-crème filling and raspberries, and finished with dusting of icing sugar. I reserve these for Fridays, as 'we fancy' on these mornings; it's a preview for the weekend and it starts the day off right!

4 day-old croissants
150g mascarpone
75g pistachio crème
Pinch of salt
150g raspberries
30g chopped pistachios
1 tbsp icing sugar, plus extra for dusting

1. Preheat the oven to 160°C Fan/180°C/350°F.
2. Slice your day-old croissants in half horizontally, but not all the way through, to create a pocket.
3. To make the pistachio-crème filling, mix together the mascarpone and pistachio-crème. Transfer into a piping bag, if you want the end result to look like something you'd get in a fancy coffee shop; if you prefer, you can very easily use a spoon instead.
4. Fill each croissant with some of the pistachio-crème and a few of the raspberries, then close and add a spoonful of the crème on top. Sprinkle with some of the chopped pistachios.
5. Bake for 4–5 minutes until the croissants are rehydrated and crispy on the outside.
6. Remove from the oven and lightly dust with icing sugar. Top with the remaining raspberries and pistachios. Best eaten warm with a nice hot cup of coffee or tea.

SERVES: 2 **PREP + COOK TIME: 5 minutes**

SPICY EGG BAGEL

These fluffy morning eggs are made in just minutes in your microwave, making them perfect for busy mornings when you want something fresh and tasty, fast. The flavour is inspired by Berber eggs, which is my daughter's favourite omelette, due to her Moroccan heritage! Served on a warm toasted bagel and topped with a drizzle of crispy chilli oil and some chopped spring onions, this dish brings a perfect balance of savoury and spicy with no effort.

4 medium eggs
Pinch of salt
Pinch of ground cumin
Pinch of paprika
1 bagel, halved and toasted

GARNISH
Drizzle of crispy chilli oil
1 spring onion, chopped

1. Take 2 small glass bowls (see Top Tip), and crack 2 eggs into each, then whisk lightly and season with the salt, cumin and paprika.

2. Place one bowl into the microwave at a time, topped with a microwave-safe lid or some cling film, and cook for 60 seconds on High. Check to see if the egg disc is cooked all the way through; you may need to give it an extra 10 seconds.

3. Remove the bowl from the microwave and, using a spoon, slowly ease the egg disc out of the bowl, take care to keep the round shape. Repeat with the other bowl of eggs.

4. Top each toasted bagel half with an egg disc, then drizzle with crispy chilli oil and scatter over the chopped spring onions. Serve immediately.

Top Tip It's important to use a glass or microwave-safe bowl that is the same circumference as your bagel, so you have the perfect ratio of bagel to egg.

MAKES: 12–16 muffins   PREP + COOK TIME: 15 minutes

GOLDEN AIR-FRYER MUFFINS

These are great to make ahead of time in preparation for busy mornings. You can use up leftover soft fruit like raspberries, strawberries and blueberries here; they will burst as they cook and turn jammy inside the muffins. With a hint of golden syrup, this is a perfect combination. You can freeze these muffins individually after baking; they defrost well.

1. Dump all the ingredients except the mixed berries and demerara sugar into a mixing bowl and stir to combine.

2. Divide the batter between 12–16 silicone muffin moulds, filling each mould two-thirds full, and place in the air-fryer basket. Depending on the size of your air fryer, you may need to work in batches.

3. Top with the mixed berries (you can alternate flavours – my daughter loves the raspberry ones and I love the blueberry ones!). Sprinkle with demerara sugar and air-fry at 160°C for 8 minutes. Every air fryer is different, so if they're not cooked enough after this time, cook for a few minutes more until the tops crack slightly. They will continue to cook after you remove them from the air fryer.

4. Let the muffins cool. You can serve them warm, or let them cool completely and store in an airtight container for up to 3 days. They also freeze well (see above).

200g self-raising flour
60g golden caster sugar
40g golden syrup
100g Greek yoghurt
2 medium eggs
75ml vegetable oil
1 tsp vanilla extract
¼ tsp salt
100g mixed berries
Demerara sugar, for topping

MAKES: 18–20 pancakes   PREP + COOK TIME: 30 minutes

FLUFFY YOGHURT PANCAKES

If anyone watches my Instagram, you'll see me batch-cook these early on Sunday mornings and place them in the freezer so I can serve them up at my leisure throughout the week. It's a dump-and-mix method that doesn't require any butter to be melted – super easy. If your mixture seems lumpy, it's no issue either, because no one has complained to me so far!

1. Add all the ingredients except the oil spray to a mixing bowl and whisk to combine – the mixture should be thick, like a cake batter.

2. Heat a non-stick frying pan over a medium heat and spray with the oil. Once the pan is hot, scoop up 1 tablespoon of batter and drop it into the pan. Repeat, trying to fit in 4 pancakes at a time. Cook for 3 minutes, or until bubbles start to appear in the batter, then flip the pancakes and cook them on the other side for another 3 minutes. If they're colouring too quickly or burning, reduce the heat.

3. Once cooked, transfer the pancakes directly to a clean tea towel to cool, covering them with the towel to allow the excess moisture to evaporate. Once cool, you can store these in a clip-seal bag for 3 days, or freeze them for later.

200g self-raising flour
150g Greek yoghurt
2 medium eggs
100ml whole milk
50g caster sugar
Pinch of salt
Avocado oil spray (or similar), for frying

Top Tip I love to serve mine with a dollop of Greek yoghurt, berries and watermelon chunks.

MAKES: 4–6 pancakes **PREP + COOK TIME: 10 minutes**

CHILLA – CHICKPEA AND SPINACH PANCAKES

Chilla are savoury Indian pancakes made with gram (besan) flour. I love the nuttiness of gram flour, and how versatile this batter is. No matter what happens, I've never made a bad chilla – they are incredibly forgiving, even if you don't measure out the ingredients accurately – so reserve these for days when you don't know what to make, because they always turn out great!

1. Mix all the ingredients except the oil spray in a mixing bowl, stirring until the lumps of chickpea flour have dissolved into the batter. You may not need all the water; start with 120ml and add more as needed until you have a smooth, pourable batter.

2. Heat a frying pan on a medium–high heat and spray it with oil. Take a ladleful of the batter and spoon it into the pan, spreading it thinly like a crêpe. As the chilla cooks, you'll see the colour change to a deep ochre, and bubbles will appear. Once it begins to dry out, flip it over and cook on the other side. This will take around 3 minutes. Repeat with the remaining batter until it's all used up. I like to spray extra oil on the chilla whilst it cooks, for added texture and colour.

3. To keep the cooked chilla soft and prevent it drying out while you fry the rest, transfer it to a plate and immediately cover with a clean tea towel.

4. I like to serve these with a dollop of coconut yoghurt and a dash of hot pepper sauce.

120g gram flour
¼ red onion, finely diced
1 tsp cumin seeds
½ tsp ground turmeric
¼ tsp ground black pepper
50g frozen spinach, defrosted, drained and finely chopped
1 green chilli, finely chopped (optional, depending on spice preference)
1 tbsp finely chopped coriander
1 tbsp finely chopped mint
120–150ml warm water
Salt, to taste
Avocado oil spray, for frying

SERVE

dollop of coconut yoghurt
hot pepper sauce, to taste

LUNCHTIME
Heroes

Lunchtime doesn't have to be stressful or time-consuming. In fact, some of the best meals are the simplest, made by just throwing together leftovers or whatever ingredients you have on hand. I think a lot of the stress comes from figuring out what to cook, but once you have that spark of inspiration, the rest falls into place.

Whether you're feeding the whole family or just yourself or the kids, these meals are designed to be simple and satisfying without any fuss. Each recipe focuses on easy-to-find, flavour-packed ingredients, with no fancy techniques or long prep times. The goal is to get wholesome, tasty meals on the table (or into lunchboxes) quickly, so you can spend less time in the kitchen and more time enjoying your meal.

SERVES: 2 **PREP + COOK TIME: 15 minutes**

CHIPOTLE CHICKEN BOWL

This easy, flavour-packed burrito bowl is cooked in the air-fryer for a perfect lunchtime treat; it also works well in lunchboxes for both adults and kids. It has the bonus of being high in protein thanks to the chicken and beans, making you feel fuller for longer.

1. Coat the chicken breasts in the chipotle paste. Spray with the oil and air-fry for 12 minutes at 180°C until the chicken is cooked through. Remove from the air fryer and set aside to rest for a few minutes.

2. Slice the chicken and divide it between two bowls. To each bowl, add half of the black beans, avocado, jalapeños and lettuce. Top with the soured cream, coriander and lime halves. If you have some tortilla chips lying around, this would be the perfect time to use them up by scattering them over the bowls for crunch!

250g skinless chicken breast fillets

2 tbsp chipotle paste

Avocado oil spray

½ x 400g tin of black beans, drained and rinsed

1 avocado, sliced

2 tsp jalapeño chilli slices, from a jar

6 lettuce leaves

2 tbsp soured cream

2 tbsp chopped coriander

1 lime, halved

Tortilla chips, to serve (optional)

SERVES: 2   PREP + COOK TIME: 15 minutes

FRESH AND CRUNCHY SUMMER ROLLS

These summer rolls are the perfect way to bring sunny vibes straight to your table. Packed with fresh veggies, fragrant herbs and whatever protein you fancy, t hey make a light and totally customisable lunch. Plus, these rolls are a great excuse to get your hands a little messy – which, let's be honest, is half the fun! My daughter loves these, and I always find that when she has had a part to play in the making of her meals, we never have an issue with eating them.

8 rice paper wrappers

8 iceberg lettuce leaves

½ cucumber, cut into large matchsticks

1 carrot, peeled and cut into matchsticks

4 sprigs of mint, leaves picked

8 sprigs of coriander

50g mangetout

1 medium firm mango, peeled and sliced into long strips

Sweet chilli sauce, to serve

1. Find a bowl big enough to fit the rice paper wrappers and fill with 5cm of cold water. Dunk in two rice paper wrappers one at a time, patting each one until it's pliable but not completely soft. Lay the wrappers flat on a chopping board, overlapping them slightly to form one large horizontal wrap.

2. Arrange two lettuce leaves over the rice paper sheets, then top with the cucumber, carrot, mint leaves, coriander, mangetout and mango.

3. Bring the bottom edge of the wrapper tightly up over the filling and then fold the sides in over it. Continue to roll up tightly from the bottom fold, place on a plate, join-side down, and cut in half on an angle. Repeat this process with the remaining ingredients. You should end up with four summer rolls altogether.

4. You can eat these straight away or place in a sealed container in the fridge to enjoy for lunch. Serve with sweet chilli sauce for the perfect pairing.

SERVES: 2   PREP + COOK TIME: 10 minutes

STICKY MUSHROOM RICE

This recipe relies on a great cheat, which is pre-cooked sticky rice! This takes the hassle out of cooking, so you can skip the waiting and dive straight into the delicious part. Whether you're at eating lunch at home or packing a lunchbox, this recipe can be made in no time, and it's the kind of meal that keeps you full and energised without the afternoon slump. Plus, it's great for kids; I like to roll this into small handheld balls that they can pop into their mouths quickly during their lunchbreak.

1. Add the mushrooms to a frying pan over a high heat and dry-fry for around 5 minutes until they begin to release their water and get some colour. Add the oil and allow the mushrooms to sizzle, then introduce the garlic and ginger and cook for 1 minute until fragrant.

2. Add the light and dark soy sauces, along with the BBQ sauce, white pepper and rice. Mix well, then cook for 2–3 minutes until all the flavours are combined into the rice. Check the flavour and see if you want to add salt.

3. Serve garnished with spring onions and a drizzle of sesame oil.

150g mixed mushrooms, finely sliced

1 tbsp vegetable oil

3 garlic cloves, finely grated

1.5cm piece of fresh ginger, finely grated

1 tbsp light soy sauce

1 tsp dark soy sauce

1 tbsp BBQ sauce

Sprinkle of white pepper

250g pouch of pre-cooked sticky rice

Salt, to taste

GARNISH

Spring onions, chopped

Drizzle of sesame oil

Top Tip If I am eating this dish on the run or making it for a packed lunch, I allow the mixture to cool after garnishing, then roll it into little balls and wrap them in cling film. If I am working from home, I fry an egg sunny-side up and add this on top, along with some crispy chilli oil.

SERVES: 4 **PREP + COOK TIME: 15 minutes**

MANGO AND HALLOUMI SHAKE-UP SALAD

This salad is a total game-changer! Packed with crispy halloumi, sweet mango and loads of fresh veggies, it's the perfect combo of flavours. The best part? You can make it a few days ahead and the dressing sits at the bottom, so when you're ready to eat, just give it a little shake and you're good to go! Super easy, super tasty and all ready when you are!

1. Spread out the halloumi cubes evenly in the air fryer basket and spray them with a little oil, then air-fry at 200°C for 6 minutes.
2. To make the dressing, place all the ingredients in a small jar, shake to combine, then divide evenly between four larger jars (I use 500ml Mason jars).
3. Divide the halloumi between the jars, followed by the mango, tomatoes, red onion, red peppers and as much lettuce as your jar can hold. Finally, top your jar with fresh herbs, leaving a small gap at the top to allow you to shake it up later. Screw the lids firmly on and place in the fridge. These will keep for up to 3 days.
4. When you're ready to eat, just shake the jar and tip out the salad on to a plate – or you can eat it straight from the jar!

200g halloumi, cut into 2cm cubes

Avocado oil spray

2 ripe mangoes, peeled and cut into 2cm chunks

75g cherry tomatoes, halved

½ red onion, finely diced

4 sprigs of mint, coarsely chopped

4 sprigs of coriander, coarsely chopped

2 pieces of roasted red pepper from a jar, sliced into rings

Iceberg lettuce, roughly chopped

DRESSING

1 tbsp honey

4 tbsp olive oil

½ tsp chilli flakes

3 tbsp apple cider vinegar

½ tsp salt

1 tsp ground black pepper

SERVES: 2

PREP + COOK TIME: 15 minutes

CRISPY RICE SALAD

My life is busy and my schedule changes from day to day, but the one thing I can always rely on is that there is rice at home! I have a thing for salty and crunchy ingredients, and using up leftover rice and transforming it into this utterly addictive crunchy addition in salads is a winner. You can make the crispy rice in advance and leave it in the fridge for up to 3 days to use when you need it.

100g leftover cooked and cooled rice (see page 10)

Avocado oil spray

½ cucumber, sliced into half-moons

¼ red cabbage, cut into long strands (see Top Tip)

¼ white cabbage, cut into long strands (see Top Tip)

75g edamame beans, fresh or frozen (see Top Tip)

½ mango, peeled and cut into small cubes

30g roasted peanuts, coarsely chopped

Chopped coriander, to garnish

DRESSING

1 tsp sesame oil

Juice of 1 lime

1 tbsp maple syrup (or honey if non-vegan)

1 tbsp soy sauce

1 tsp rice vinegar

Salt and ground white pepper, to taste

1. To make the crispy rice, place the leftover rice into the air-fryer basket and spray with oil, then mix with your hands. Air-fry for 6–8 minutes at 200°C until the rice is crispy.

2. Place all the ingredients for the dressing in a small jar and shake it up to combine.

3. Add all the vegetables to a bowl, along with the mango and peanuts, and pour over the dressing. I always love mixing my salad using my hands, because you can ensure every part of the salad is covered with dressing.

4. Tumble the crispy rice over the salad and toss to combine. Scatter over some coriander and serve immediately.

Top Tip To prepare the cabbage, I use a speed peeler, which leaves you with long strands of cut cabbage.

If using frozen edamame beans, pop them in a bowl and pour over some hot water, then let sit for 3 minutes. Drain, and then use.

SERVES: 1 **PREP + COOK TIME: 5 minutes**

SPICY TUNA AND CUCUMBER SALAD

Last summer I had this on repeat every day for two months! It's the perfect combination of crunchy and fresh flavours. The cucumber balances the heat of the chilli, and it's a quick and flavourful meal to eat on the go or as a light lunch option. Be warned, this is addictive!

160g tin of tuna (preferably in spring water), drained

2 tbsp mayonnaise

1–2 tbsp sriracha (depending on your preference)

1 tsp soy sauce

½ tsp sesame oil

1 tsp rice vinegar

3 baby cucumbers, or ½ standard cucumber, thinly sliced

Handful of jalapeño slices from a jar

GARNISH (OPTIONAL)

Sprinkle of sesame seeds

1 spring onion, green part only, chopped

1 nori sheet, crumbled

1. In a bowl, fork up the tuna to break it into pieces, making sure it still has some texture.

2. Add the mayo, sriracha, soy sauce, sesame oil and rice vinegar and stir to combine, then taste for the right flavour balance, adjusting as needed.

3. Add the sliced cucumber and jalapeños. Finish by adding the optional garnishes, or eat it just as it is.

SERVES: 2–4   PREP + COOK TIME: 15 minutes

CREAMY COCONUT TOMATO DAAL

While this is perfect for lunch, it has also been a game-changer for whenever I have no time to cook and my brain can't think of any other options. I find so much comfort in daal, and love how speedy and nutritious this meal is. It's packed with fibre and protein, so it will certainly hit the spot and keep you going for the rest of the afternoon. This transports easily in a hot flask for packed lunches; I normally pop some rice in the bottom and ladle over some daal, and it stays warm, ready to provide immediate comfort.

1. Tip the red lentils into a sieve and rinse under cold water until the water runs clear.
2. Add the drained lentils to a large microwave-safe bowl and top with all the other ingredients. Microwave on High for 8–10 minutes, stopping halfway to stir the lentils.
3. After cooking, stir again to encourage the lentils and tomatoes to break up; the more you do this, the creamier your daal will become.
4. Garnish your daal with coriander and serve with roti, naan, or rice, or just as it is.

150g dried red lentils

400ml tin of full-fat coconut milk

1 vegetable stock cube, crumbled

1 tsp tomato paste

50g cherry tomatoes, cut into quarters

1 tsp garam masala

1 tsp ground cumin

½ tsp ground turmeric

Salt, to taste

SERVE

Chopped coriander

Roti, naan or rice, (optional)

SERVES: 2–4   PREP + COOK TIME: 25 minutes

HARISSA ROASTED PUMPKIN AND CHICKPEAS

One of my favourite life hacks is that you don't have to peel the pumpkin! Just cook the skin and eat it. Trust me, life is much better when you skip this step; the skin becomes tender and delicious, and adds extra fibre and texture to the dish. The best part about this recipe is that it's all cooked in the air fryer, so it's perfect when you are working from home – you can even make this the night before and eat it cold the next day, as the flavours will have had time to sit together and become friends!

600g pumpkin, skin on, deseeded and cut into cubes

400g tin of chickpeas, drained and rinsed

1 tbsp olive oil

2 tbsp harissa paste

1 tsp ground cumin

1 tsp paprika

1 tsp garlic granules

Salt, to taste

SERVE

Chopped coriander, to garnish

Couscous, to serve (optional)

1. Add the pumpkin cubes and chickpeas to the air fryer. Add the oil, harissa paste and all the spices, and toss to evenly coat, then arrange in a single layer.

2. Air-fry at 200°C for 15–20 minutes, shaking the basket halfway through, until the pumpkin is tender and slightly caramelised and the chickpeas are crispy.

3. Serve with couscous and garnished with coriander, or just as it is.

MAKES: 6–8 fritters   PREP + COOK TIME: 10–15 minutes

SPICY SWEETCORN FRITTERS

These fritters are the perfect lunch when you're short on time but still want something tasty and hot. They are foolproof, and you can use tinned or frozen sweetcorn depending on what you have. All you have to do is mix everything together, spoon the batter into a hot pan, and in just a few minutes you've got fritters that are golden and crispy, quick and light.

1. In a medium bowl, combine the sweetcorn, rice and gram flours, baking powder, spring onions, chilli, coriander, Chinese 5 spice, soy sauce, water and salt, and mix until well combined. The mixture should resemble a thick cake batter.

2. Heat the oil in a large saucepan over a medium–high heat. Add 2 tablespoons of the mixture to create a fritter, then continue adding more, depending on how much space you have. Usually you can cook these in batches of 3–4, cooking for 3–4 minutes on each side.

3. Once cooked, transfer the fritters to a plate lined with kitchen paper to absorb some of the oil, and set aside whilst you make the rest. I serve these hot, with a large dollop of Greek yoghurt mixed with sriracha.

- 340g tinned or frozen sweetcorn kernels
- 50g rice flour
- 50g gram flour
- ½ tsp baking powder
- 2–3 spring onions, finely chopped
- 1 small red chilli, finely chopped
- 4 sprigs of coriander, chopped
- 1 tsp Chinese 5 spice
- 1 tsp soy sauce
- 150ml warm water
- 3–4 tbsp vegetable oil, for frying (enough to cover the pan)
- Salt, to taste
- Greek yoghurt mixed with sriracha (optional)

SERVES: 2 **PREP + COOK TIME: 15 minutes**

SUSHI RICE WAFFLE, TOMATOES AND A CRISPY CHILLI OIL

If you've got leftover sushi rice, don't throw it away! I know from experience that families often end up with extra rice after a meal, and instead of letting it go to waste, you can easily turn it into sushi waffles. It's a great way to repurpose those leftover grains! I absolutely need a kick of chilli at lunchtime, and I love the contrast of the punchy chilli and crisp tomato salad with crunchy, hot sushi rice.

300g leftover sushi rice (see page 10)

1 tbsp vegetable oil

2 tbsp light soy sauce

180g baby plum tomatoes, halved

½ red onion, sliced into half-moons

1 tsp rice vinegar

1 tsp sesame oil

1 tbsp crispy chilli oil

½ tsp salt

Handful of coriander, chopped

Squeeze of lime juice

1. Mix the leftover rice with the oil and soy sauce. Spoon the rice into a waffle iron, pressing it evenly. Don't overfill, as you want the rice to crisp up.
2. In a bowl, combine the rest of the ingredients.
3. When the waffle is cooked, tumble the tomato mixture over the top and eat straight away.

Top Tip I use a waffle iron for this recipe, but don't worry if you don't have one – these can be made in a pan in the same way as you would make pancakes.

ALL IN
One Pot

You know why I love one-pot cooking so much? Because on those days when I'm totally wiped out, when my daughter and I are rushing around, or it's freezing outside, or I'm just exhausted, one-pot cooking is such a lifesaver. It's the dump-it-all-in method, meaning you don't have to give it too much thought – but the best part is that one-pot cooking doesn't mean everything tastes the same. You can still create layers of flavour and add texture if you know how to time it right. I'm going to show you how to do just that, so even on your busiest and most tiring days you can enjoy a dish that's full of depth and flavour, and not a one-texture experience. These recipes are comforting and satisfying, without all the stress or the clean-up. Well, to be honest, you should be letting the others do the clean-up by now!

SERVES: 4–6 **PREP + COOK TIME: 30 minutes**

GREEN BIRIYANI

This is a vegan version of my much-loved Mauritian briani. In Mauritius, our brianis are light and fragrant, but it's hard to come across a vegan version. I made this for my meat-loving 6-foot-four nephew and he ate everything; I don't know whether he liked it more than the meat version, but he certainly didn't complain. This is the best way to get a briani fix when you are up against it timewise. It's nourishing and comforting, and we always have a little left over, which I love to eat with extra chilli when I'm working from home the next day!

1. Place all the ingredients, excluding the rice and water, into a wide saucepan with a lid, mixing the vegetables with the yoghurt and spices until thoroughly covered – I find it easiest to use my hands here. Press down to create an even layer. Top with the rice, making sure it's even, then cover with the water.

2. Bring the pan to a roaring boil and quickly cover with a tight-fitting lid. As soon as the lid is on, reduce the heat to a simmer. Cook with the lid on for 12 minutes.

3. After 12 minutes, turn off the heat but do not remove the lid. Allow the rice and vegetables to sit for at least 10 minutes. You can leave this to sit and stay warm for up to 1 hour.

4. When you're ready to eat, fork up the rice and serve warm, garnished with the chopped coriander, onions and chilli.

200g cassava, chopped into 5cm pieces (I use frozen)
100g frozen peas
200g broccoli cut into florets (fresh or frozen)
150g coconut yoghurt
2 tbsp garam masala
1 tbsp garlic and ginger paste
1 vegetable stock cube
1 cinnamon stick
1 tsp cumin seeds
6 cloves
2 cardamom pods, crushed
½ tsp ground turmeric
1 tsp salt
400g basmati rice (I use extra-long basmati)
600ml cold water

GARNISH
1 tbsp chopped coriander
1 tbsp fried onions
1 large red chilli, sliced

SERVES: 4   PREP + COOK TIME: 35 minutes

SALMON TERIYAKI RICE

I made this with the legendary Chef Kamol, an enthusiastic home cook who began his career as an Instagram legend at the age of nine! He is such an inspiration to me, and he makes the most delicious meals for his little brother Salahudin, often cooking alongside his dear grandma. I love watching his videos because it reminds me that we all need inspiration for midweek family meals. We cooked this together in his kitchen in London, and it was true perfection!

4 salmon fillets (120g each), butterflied (see Top Tip)
150g broccoli florets
½ red pepper, sliced
½ yellow pepper, sliced

RICE
250g sushi rice, washed
400ml water
1 tsp salt

DRESSING
1 tbsp garlic and ginger paste
1 tsp sesame oil
2 tbsp honey
1 tsp rice vinegar
2 tbsp soy sauce (or tamari for gluten-free)
½ tsp salt

GARNISH
Drizzle of sesame oil
Small sprinkle of black and white sesame seeds
1 spring onion, green part only, finely chopped

1. Place the rice, water and salt into a pan, then cover and cook over a medium heat for 8 minutes.
2. Make the dressing by stirring together all the ingredients in a jug, then set aside.
3. Once the rice has cooked for 8 minutes, lay the salmon flat over the top of the rice and scatter the broccoli and peppers around it. Drizzle the dressing over the top, then pop the lid back on and steam over a medium–low heat for a further 8 minutes.
4. Turn off the heat and allow the fish and rice to sit for 10 minutes, still covered.
5. Remove the lid, drizzle over some sesame oil, scatter over the sesame seeds and spring onions, and serve.

Top Tip To 'butterfly' the salmon, just slice it down the centre horizontally, to create two fillets.

SERVES: 4–6 **PREP + COOK TIME: 25 minutes**

CREAMY GARLIC CHICKEN PASTA

This is one of those dishes that's perfect for cold nights when you just need something quick and cosy. With eight cloves of garlic – yes, you heard me right! – and a little hint of chilli, it's packed with flavour and has just the right amount of kick. The pasta and chicken cook together in one pot all at the same time. I usually pair it with some broccoli on the side, just to get a bit of green in there. It's a go-to meal that's simple, filling and always a hit with all ages.

1. Heat the olive oil in a saucepan over a medium–high heat. Add the chicken, season with salt and pepper and fry off for about 5 minutes to brown.

2. Add the garlic and spices and sauté for a few minutes, then toss in the rigatoni, cream and chicken stock. Bring to a boil, reduce the heat to medium–low and cook for 15 minutes with the lid on.

3. Check the pasta after 8 minutes: give it a stir and see if it requires additional water. You can add 50–100ml extra depending on how saucy you want it.

4. Once the pasta is al dente, turn off the heat, stir in the Parmesan and check for seasoning. Finish with the lemon zest, chopped coriander or parsley and extra Parmesan, to serve.

2 tbsp olive oil

400g skinless, boneless chicken thighs, cut into 2cm cubes

8 garlic cloves, finely chopped, or 2 heaped tbsp garlic paste

1 tbsp smoked paprika

1 tsp dried chilli flakes

1 tsp ground white pepper

300g dried rigatoni

250ml double cream

400ml chicken stock (I use one stock cube)

50g Parmesan, grated, plus extra to serve

Salt and ground black pepper, to taste

SERVE

Zest of ½ lemon

Handful of chopped coriander or parsley

SERVES: 4–6 PREP + COOK TIME: 30 minutes

MAURITIAN MOON FAN BRAISED CHICKEN RICE

For me, this is the most comforting one-pot chicken and rice out there: a classic Sino–Mauritian (Chinese) dish that's made by many islanders. It's typically served alongside a salad, chutney and, in true Mauritian spirit, a tiny hot chilli called pima confit. I don't expect you to make all the sides when you're rushed for time, so a drizzle of some crispy chilli oil and a green salad will suffice!

1. In a bowl, mix the chicken with the garlic and ginger paste, black pepper, oyster sauce and both soy sauces, then set aside.
2. In a large saucepan over a medium heat, fry off the sausage for 2 minutes on each side, until some of the oil is drawn out and it becomes crispy. Transfer the sausage to a plate, leaving the oil in the pan.
3. Add the onion, seasoned chicken and sliced mushrooms to the pan and fry until they become caramelised – this will take about 5–7 minutes.
4. Add the washed jasmine rice and top with the chicken stock. Bring to the boil, then reduce the heat to a simmer, cover with a tight-fitting lid and steam for around 12 minutes.
5. Turn off the heat, remove the lid and fluff up the rice with a fork. Top with the sliced sausage, scatter over the spring onions and serve straight away. You can keep the lid on and it will stay hot with the residual heat of the pan for up to 1 hour.

6 skinless, boneless chicken thighs, cut into 10cm pieces
1 heaped tbsp garlic and ginger paste
1 tsp ground black pepper
2 tbsp oyster sauce
1 tbsp dark soy sauce
1 tbsp light soy sauce
80g Chinese sausage, sliced (see Top Tip)
½ white onion, coarsely diced
80g shiitake mushrooms, finely sliced
300g jasmine rice, washed and drained
550ml chicken stock
3 spring onions, green parts only, finely sliced

Top Tip If you can't get hold of Chinese sausage, you could use salami or chorizo. I don't eat pork, so I use a brilliant halal smoked turkey and beef sausage.

SERVES: 3–4   PREP + COOK TIME: 10 minutes

MAURITIAN NOODLES

This recipe reminds me of sitting with my feet in the sand at Belle Mare, a beach on Mauritius, enjoying these noodles from a take-away container doused with a heavy portion of garlic water with which we typically serve this dish, and a large dollop of chilli paste. The most important part of this recipe is preparation! Get your sauce ready first, then everything else falls into place effortlessly. You can grab pre-cooked noodles for extra convenience; then it's all about tossing in whatever veggies you have to hand for a delicious, no-waste meal that is ready in minutes. I get my daughter to do the veg prep with me, and it comes together like a dream!

3 tbsp vegetable oil

4 spring onions, cut into 5cm pieces

150g baby corn, halved on the diagonal

1 large carrot, julienned

200g pak choi, chopped

400g pre-cooked noodles (or 300g dried noodles, cooked)

20g fresh chives, cut into 5cm pieces

Drizzle of sesame oil, to finish

SAUCE

1 tbsp oyster sauce (or vegetarian alternative)

2 tbsp soy sauce

1 tbsp dark soy sauce

1 tsp white caster sugar

1 tbsp garlic and ginger paste

1 tsp ground white pepper

1. Make the sauce by stirring together all the ingredients in a jug, then set aside.

2. Heat half the vegetable oil in a large saucepan over a high heat. Add the spring onions, baby corn, carrot and pak choi, and fry for 2–3 minutes, until just softened, then remove from the pan and set aside.

3. Add the remaining oil to the pan and toss in the noodles. Fry for 2–3 minutes, stirring so that the noodles separate, then return the veggies to the pan. Pour in the sauce and fry it all together for a few more minutes.

4. Turn off the heat, sprinkle over the chives and drizzle over some sesame oil to finish.

Top Tip I like to serve this with my chilli sauce (see page 157).

SERVES: 4–6 PREP + COOK TIME: 25 minutes

BLACK BEAN STEW WITH PLANTAIN

The balance of sweet, salty and savoury notes makes this dish so satisfying. The only issue I have with this recipe is that plantain isn't as cheap as it once was. I used to be able to get four plantains for £1 back in Tooting Market in my youth; now you'll be lucky to get two at that price! Using black beans is a great way to bulk out this recipe, adding extra protein and fibre. Trust me, you'll be coming back for seconds!

2 tbsp olive oil

1 onion, diced

3 garlic cloves, minced

1 small Scotch bonnet chilli, finely chopped (optional)

1 tbsp smoked paprika

1 tsp ground cumin

Sprig of thyme

2 x 400g tins of black beans, drained and rinsed

400ml tin of full-fat coconut milk

250ml vegetable stock

2 ripe plantains, peeled and sliced

1 red pepper, diced

Juice of 1 lime

Salt and black pepper, to taste

Fresh coriander, for garnish

1. Heat the olive oil in a large saucepan over a medium heat. Add the onion and garlic and fry until fragrant, around 3 minutes.
2. Add the Scotch bonnet, smoked paprika, cumin and thyme. Cook for another minute to release the flavours.
3. Add the black beans, coconut milk, stock and plantains, and cook for another 10 minutes until the plantain is tender.
4. Stir in the red pepper, season and cook for a further 5 minutes,
5. Take the stew off the heat and stir in the lime juice. Serve garnished with coriander.

Top Tip At home, we normally have blue corn chips on the side to dip into the stew for some texture – or you can make this meal stretch to 8 people if you serve it with rice.

SERVES: 4–6 PREP + COOK TIME: 30 minutes

CHICKEN BULGUR PILAF

This dish is everything you want in a weeknight meal – warm, hearty and packed with rich, comforting flavours. The tender chicken melts in your mouth, while the bulgur soaks up all the delicious chicken juices and spices, making this incredibly comforting. What really makes this dish special is the Baharat spice blend, a Middle Eastern blend that you can get in the spice aisle of your supermarket. A fragrant mix of warm spices like cinnamon, cardamom and cumin, it brings a deep, earthy richness with just a hint of sweetness. I like to serve this pilaf with my Honeyed Carrots (see page 160).

1. Heat the olive oil in a large saucepan over a medium heat. Add the chicken, season with salt and pepper, and cook, skin-side down, until golden brown (about 5 minutes). Remove to a plate and set aside.

2. In the same pan, cook the onion until soft. Stir in the garlic, Baharat spice blend, paprika and turmeric, then cook for a further 1 minute until fragrant.

3. Add the bulgur wheat, tomato paste and chicken stock, stirring well. Return the chicken to the pan and bring to a gentle simmer, then cover and cook over a low heat for 15–20 minutes until the bulgur absorbs the liquid and becomes tender. Once cooked, fluff up with a fork and adjust the seasoning if needed.

4. Garnish with parsley and serve with lemon wedges.

2 tbsp olive oil
500g boneless chicken thighs, skin on
1 onion, finely chopped
2 garlic cloves, minced
2 tbsp Baharat spice blend
1 tbsp smoked paprika
½ tsp ground turmeric
250g bulgur wheat
1 tbsp tomato paste
450ml chicken stock (I use 1 stock cube)
Salt and black pepper, to taste
Chopped parsley, to garnish
Lemon wedges, to serve

SERVES: 4   PREP + COOK TIME: 30 minutes

LAMB MEATBALL RED THAI CURRY

This dish is a guaranteed crowd-pleaser! Juicy, flavourful lamb meatballs simmered in a rich, creamy, coconut-based red Thai curry: it's the perfect balance of sweet and savoury, and has just the right amount of spice. The lemongrass adds a fresh, zesty twist, while a topping of fragrant basil brings everything together beautifully. The kids love it because it's a little spicy and creamy, but I love it because I can add some chilli for that extra kick. You can serve it with noodles, rice or linguine for a comforting, satisfying meal that feels like a treat but is easy enough for any night of the week!

1. Fry the meatballs in a dry saucepan over a medium heat for about 5 minutes until browned on all sides. Remove to a plate and set aside, keeping the residual oil in the pan.
2. Add the garlic and ginger paste, red Thai curry paste and lemongrass paste to the same pan and cook for 1–2 minutes until fragrant.
3. Pour in the coconut milk, chicken stock, fish sauce and brown sugar. Stir well and bring to a gentle simmer. Taste here to check the balance of flavours – you can add more or less of the seasonings to get the perfect balance of sweet, sour, salty and hot.
4. Return the meatballs to the pan and let everything simmer for 15 minutes until the meatballs are fully cooked and the sauce has thickened. Add the red pepper for the final 5 minutes of cooking. Turn off the heat and stir in the basil and lime juice.
5. Serve hot with your preferred accompaniment.

350g ready-made lamb meatballs (12 balls)
1 tbsp garlic and ginger paste
2 tbsp red Thai curry paste
1 tsp lemongrass paste
400ml tin of full-fat coconut milk
250ml chicken stock (I use a stock cube)
1 tbsp fish sauce
1 tbsp brown sugar
1 red pepper, sliced
25g basil leaves
Juice of 1 lime

SERVES: 4   PREP + COOK TIME: 20 minutes

CAJUN SEAFOOD STEW

This freezer-raid meal is vibrant and flavour-packed, bringing a little tropical warmth to your table! Juicy prawns, tender fish and plump mussels are gently cooked in a light yet creamy coconut broth, making every spoonful rich but not heavy. Sweetcorn and sweet potato add a natural sweetness that perfectly balances the dish, giving it a deliciously comforting twist.

- 200g frozen king prawns
- 300g frozen cod fillets, or any other white fish (such as tilapia or haddock)
- 250g frozen mussels
- 150g frozen sweetcorn
- 250g frozen sweet potato chunks
- 400ml tin of full-fat coconut milk
- 400ml vegetable or fish stock
- 2 tbsp Cajun seasoning
- 1 tsp vegetable bouillon powder
- 3 garlic cloves, minced
- 1 red pepper, cut into 2cm chunks
- 2 spring onions, cut into thirds
- 1 red chilli, finely chopped
- Juice of 1 lime
- Salt and black pepper, to taste
- 4 sprigs of coriander, chopped, to serve

1. In a medium saucepan, combine the frozen prawns, white fish, mussels, sweetcorn, sweet potato chunks, coconut milk, stock, Cajun seasoning, bouillon powder and garlic. Bring to the boil, then reduce to a simmer and cook for 5 minutes.

2. Add the red pepper, spring onions, chilli and lime juice. Check the seasoning and cook for 3 minutes more.

3. Once cooked, garnish with fresh coriander and serve.

Top Tip Feel free to use prawns with the heads on or off, and mussels with or without their shells. I love to keep them on to add an extra depth of flavour to the dish.

SERVES: 4 **PREP + COOK TIME: 10 minutes**

MAURITIAN ROTI BEEF

This quick and flavourful Creole-inspired stir-fry is perfect for busy weeknights. With just a handful of ingredients and minimal prep, it comes together in under 10 minutes. The rich, aromatic sauce made with star anise, soy, ginger and garlic makes this dish deeply comforting. While traditionally made with beef, it works just as well with sliced chicken breast or firm tofu. Best served with a crusty baguette to soak up all the pan juices! I love to serve this with my Mauritian Chilli Sauce (page 157), too.

2 tbsp vegetable oil (or any other neutral oil)

500g ribeye or sirloin steak, thinly sliced

1 tbsp garlic and ginger paste

2 star anise

3 tbsp soy sauce (or tamari for gluten-free)

1 tbsp oyster sauce (or gluten-free alternative)

1 tsp caster sugar

1 tsp ground black pepper

1 small onion, sliced

1 small red chilli, sliced (optional)

Chopped coriander, to garnish

100ml water (optional)

SERVE

Crusty baguette, to serve (optional)

1. Heat the oil in a wok or large frying pan over a high heat. Once hot, add the beef, garlic and ginger paste and star anise, and sear the meat until browned.

2. Add the soy sauce, oyster sauce, sugar, black pepper, onion and chilli, if using, then cook for another 1–2 minutes. If you want to create more sauce, you can add the water and let it cook down for a few minutes more. I like mine on the drier side of saucy!

3. Garnish with fresh coriander and serve hot.

SERVES: 4–6　　　　PREP + COOK TIME: 35 minutes

TURKISH LAMB AND AUBERGINE TRAYBAKE

This dish is as stunning to look at as it is delicious to eat! Usually made with fresh lamb meatballs, this cheat's version uses ready-made meatballs, which makes all the difference in getting this on the table speedily! Tender lamb, soft aubergine and golden potatoes are layered in a gorgeous spiral, with pops of colourful peppers in between. Everything is bathed in a rich, garlicky red pepper and tomato sauce, then brightened with lemon and a hint of smoky paprika. As it bakes, the flavours meld together, creating a hearty, comforting meal that's perfect for sharing. Serve it with warm bread or pitta bread to scoop up every bit – because trust me, you won't want to waste a drop!

1. Flatten the meatballs between your hands until they are the same thickness as the potatoes and aubergines.
2. Preheat the oven to 180°C fan/200°C/400°F. Arrange the meatballs, potatoes, aubergines and peppers in a circular pattern in a round baking dish.
3. In a bowl, combine the olive oil, chicken stock, tomato paste, paprika, cumin, pepper, garlic granules, sugar, salt and lemon juice, then pour this sauce evenly over the top of the meatballs and vegetables.
4. Cover with foil and bake in the oven for 15 minutes. Remove the foil, then bake for another 10 minutes, until everything is golden and bubbling. Serve immediately.

350g ready-made gluten-free lamb meatballs (12 balls)

3 potatoes (about 500g), sliced into 1cm rounds

2 aubergines (about 500g), sliced into 1cm rounds

1 red and 1 yellow pepper, sliced

2 tbsp olive oil

300ml chicken stock (I use stock cubes)

2 tbsp Turkish tomato paste

1 tbsp smoked paprika

1 tsp ground cumin

1 tsp ground black pepper

1 tsp garlic granules

½ tsp caster sugar

1 tsp salt

Juice of 1 lemon

SERVES: 4–6   PREP + COOK TIME: 45 minutes

CHICKEN JOLLOF

Jollof is my all-time comfort dish – no debate. My best friend Bola knows this, and her sister Shade's jollof is legendary: always rich, smoky and packed with flavour, and each grain of rice is singular and defined. She always makes it for big parties. I can see Shade roll her eyes at this recipe, but this version is a one-pot wonder, with the chicken cooked right on top, soaking up all that spicy, tomato-infused goodness. And as for where the best jollof comes from? I'm staying out of that debate, because I will not be finished off that way! I hold up my hands to the fact that this is not the traditional recipe, but I know it will keep me comforted until I get fed the real deal by my friends.

1. Rub the chicken with the salt, pepper, paprika, garlic granules and 1 teaspoon of the bouillon powder.

2. Heat the oil in a large pan over a high heat, then brown the chicken on all sides for about 5 minutes. Remove the chicken and set aside, keeping the residual oils in the pan.

3. Add the onion, tomatoes, red pepper and Scotch bonnet to a blender, and blend to a paste. Add this to the pan, along with the tomato paste, and cook until the mixture thickens and darkens – this should take 5–7 minutes. Stir often to make sure it doesn't burn.

4. Add the bay leaf, rice, chicken stock, remaining bouillon powder and a pinch of salt. Make sure this is all stirred together thoroughly. Lay the chicken over the rice and cover the pan with a tight-fitting lid. Reduce the heat to a simmer and let it cook for about 30 minutes.

5. Remove the pan from the heat and let it rest for a few minutes before fluffing the rice with a fork. You can put the chicken into the air fryer to crisp up again if you like, or just serve it as it is.

6 boneless chicken thighs, skin on

½ tsp salt, plus extra to taste

½ tsp ground black pepper

1 tsp paprika

1 tsp garlic granules

1 tbsp vegetable bouillon powder

4 tbsp vegetable oil

½ large onion, roughly chopped

2 tomatoes, roughly chopped

1 red pepper, roughly chopped

1 Scotch bonnet chilli, sliced

4 tbsp Turkish tomato paste

1 bay leaf

400g sella basmati rice (I use golden sella basmati, or grand extra-long), washed

300ml chicken stock

Top Tip I like to serve this with my Mauritian chilli sauce (see page 157).

WHIP IT UP
in 15

I know how it goes – work, school, life ... and suddenly it's dinnertime, and you've got zero energy to cook. But trust me, you don't need to spend hours in the kitchen to put a proper meal on the table. This chapter is all about speedy, smart shortcuts, quick hacks and recipes that might seem a little wild at first but will seriously change the game for you. Also, these are meals that you can easily teach the youngsters to master, so it's a great way to introduce them to cooking!

SERVES: 4   PREP + COOK TIME: 15 minutes

PRAWNS IN CREOLE SAUCE

This dish is a total game-changer, packed with bold flavours and so easy to make! The best part? It's incredibly versatile. Toss the sauce with pasta, spoon it over rice, scoop it up with roti or even stuff it into a fluffy jacket potato. Once you get the hang of making a classic Mauritian Creole sauce, you'll find yourself using it in all sorts of delicious ways. The juicy, sweet prawns soak up the rich spiced tomato sauce beautifully, with just the right kick of heat to keep things exciting.

1. Heat the oil in a large pan over a high heat. Add the spring onions, garlic and ginger paste, chillies, coriander stems and thyme sprig, and cook for 2 minutes until fragrant.

2. Add the tomatoes, paprika and sugar, then stir and allow to soften for around 5 minutes – you will need to crush the tomatoes a little to encourage them to break down. Season with salt and pepper, then add the prawns. Cook for 3–4 minutes until the prawns turn pink and opaque. Be careful not to overcook them.

3. Turn off the heat and sprinkle over the coriander leaves just before serving.

2 tbsp vegetable oil

2 spring onions, snipped into pieces

1 tbsp garlic and ginger paste

2 red chillies, slit in half with the seeds left in

1 tbsp finely chopped coriander stems, leaves reserved for garnish

Sprig of thyme

6 plum tomatoes, quatered

1 tsp smoky sweet paprika

1 tsp white caster sugar

500g raw prawns (see Top Tip)

Salt and black pepper, to taste

Top Tip You can leave the shells on the prawns for extra flavour, or remove them if you don't want the mess when eating.

SERVES: 4   **PREP + COOK TIME: 10 minutes**

PINEAPPLE FRIED RICE WITH CASHEWS

This is one of those magical dishes that turns simple ingredients into something super delicious! Sweet, tangy pineapple, fragrant ginger and crunchy cashews come together in a quick and easy one-pan meal. It's perfect for using up leftover rice and totally customisable, so feel free to add your favourite protein if you have some lying around in the fridge.

2 tbsp vegetable oil

1 tbsp garlic and ginger paste

3 spring onions, sliced, white and green parts separated

1–2 small red chillies (depending on how hot you want it), finely chopped

100g cashews

500g leftover cooked jasmine rice (or use 2 x 250g pre-cooked pouches)

200g tin of chopped pineapple, drained

2 tbsp soy sauce

1 tsp Chinese 5 spice

1 tsp ground white pepper

½ tsp salt

Drizzle of sesame oil

GARNISH

1 tsp black and white sesame seeds

Handful of coriander or basil leaves

1 lime, quartered

1. In a large frying pan or wok, heat the oil over a medium–high heat. Add the garlic and ginger paste, spring onion whites, chillies and cashews, and stir-fry for about 30 seconds until fragrant.

2. Add the rice, breaking up any clumps, and stir-fry for 2–3 minutes.

3. Toss in the pineapple pieces, soy sauce, Chinese 5 spice, white pepper and salt, and cook for 1 minute to heat through. Drizzle over the sesame oil, then remove from the heat and mix in the spring onion greens.

4. Garnish with sesame seeds and fresh coriander or basil, and serve with lime wedges for squeezing.

TUNA SUUGO WITH BAASTA

SERVES: 4–6
PREP + COOK TIME: 15 minutes

Years ago, while working on a community project in Southampton, I had the pleasure of meeting some Somali women who introduced me to the magic of xawaash, the Somali equivalent of garam masala. They made a simple yet flavourful suugo (sauce), which they paired with tuna and baasta (pasta). The influence of Italian cuisine in Somalia is evident in suugo, creating a fusion that is distinctly Somalian but has spiced up my midweek menu at home. The traditional way is to serve this with banana, but that's up to you. It was my first time experiencing the unique combination of banana with a savoury dish, and I was immediately hooked!

300g dried spaghetti

2 x 125g tins of tuna in oil

½ large onion, finely chopped

4 garlic cloves, finely minced or grated

400g tin of chopped tomatoes

2 tbsp Turkish tomato paste

1 tsp white caster sugar

1–2 tsp xawaash spice blend (depending on taste)

Salt and black pepper, to taste

GARNISH (OPTIONAL)

Chopped coriander or parsley

Banana

1. Bring a large pot of salted water to the boil. Add the spaghetti and cook according to the package instructions. Drain, reserving some of the cooking water.

2. Drain the tuna oil into a frying pan over a medium–high heat. Add the onion and a sprinkle of salt, and cook for a few minutes until the onion begins to soften. Then add in the garlic and cook for 1 minute more until fragrant.

3. Add the chopped tomatoes, tomato paste, sugar and xawaash spice blend, then increase the heat to high and cook for around 15 minutes until the oil comes to the surface. Keep stirring to help the tomatoes soften. Add the drained tuna, then season with salt and pepper.

4. Once the sauce is ready, add the cooked spaghetti to the pan and toss gently to coat it in the sauce. Use some of the reserved pasta water to loosen the sauce, if needed.

5. Serve the suugo and tuna spaghetti hot, garnished with fresh coriander or parsley, with a banana on the side of the plate.

Top Tip I usually source my xawaash from my local international supermarket. If you can't find it there, Garam Masala will work as a good substitute.

SERVES: 4   PREP + COOK TIME: 15 minutes

PARATHA CHILLI-CHEESE ROLLS

Frozen parathas are a total lifesaver; flaky, buttery and ready in minutes. These are my go-to on swimming nights. I wrap them in foil and they're eaten warm in the car on the way home. Quick, satisfying and delicious! You can use whatever you have in the fridge, but I love the combination of cheese, chilli and onion here.

1. In a small bowl, combine the garlic granules, mozzarella, chillies and spring onions. Season with salt and pepper and set aside.
2. Heat a frying pan over a medium heat and cook a paratha for 2–3 minutes until golden brown on both sides. Set aside to keep warm, and repeat until you have cooked all the parathas.
3. Sprinkle the cheese mixture evenly over the four cooked parathas while the wraps are still warm. Wrap them tightly in foil to make a parcel.
4. At this stage, you can pop them in the fridge, then air-fry them whenever you want to eat them. Alternatively, you can return them to the pan and cook them with the foil on for around 2 minutes, until the cheese has melted. Turn them a few times to ensure they heat through evenly.
5. Pop these into a container, jump in the car and head to your after-school activities with warm chilli-cheese parathas to keep you going!

1 tsp garlic granules

150g mozzarella, grated

1–2 green chillies (depending on how hot you want it), finely chopped

2 spring onions, finely sliced

4 frozen parathas

Salt and black pepper, to taste

SERVES: 4 **PREP + COOK TIME: 15 minutes**

TURKISH PIZZA BREAD

When midweek madness hits (which is a regular occurrence at my house) and I need dinner on the table fast, having this cheat's lahmacun, or Turkish pizza, in my armoury makes everything so easy. It's my go-to when I want something packed with flavour but without the fuss. I use khobz bread as a shortcut, which you can now get in supermarkets, but you can use any flatbread or even tortillas. Just spread them with this spiced lamb mixture and pop them under the grill for a few minutes until crispy. My daughter takes charge with making the salad, and in total this takes less than 15 minutes. Everyone loves loading theirs up with fresh herbs, salad, chilli and a squeeze of lemon.

1. Preheat the grill to high.
2. Place the mince in a bowl with the onion, garlic granules, tomato paste, Baharat spice mix and chilli flakes. Season with salt and pepper, and mix thoroughly.
3. Place the knobz or tortilla wraps on baking trays. Spread the spiced lamb mixture thinly over each one, so that it reaches the edges of the bread, pressing it down slightly. Pop each lahmacun under the grill for 3–5 minutes, or until the edges are golden and crispy.
4. Sprinkle with chopped tomatoes, cucumber, red onion, parsley and sumac, drizzle over some lemon juice, then roll and eat! Serve with some lemon wedges alongside, if you like.

300g lamb mince

1 small onion, grated

1 tsp garlic granules

1 tbsp Turkish tomato paste

1 tbsp Baharat spice mix

½-2 tsp chilli flakes (adjust according to taste)

4 large khobz or tortilla wraps

2 tomatoes, finely chopped

¼ cucumber, finely chopped

½ red onion, thinly sliced

Small handful of parsley, chopped

1 tsp sumac

Juice of ½ lemon, plus wedges to serve (optional)

Salt and black pepper, to taste

SERVES: 4 **PREP + COOK TIME: 15 minutes**

CEVAPI – JUICY GRILLED BALKAN KEBABS

Mladen, my sister-in-law's father, makes the best cevapi, we've eaten our fair share over the years! These juicy, flavour-packed grilled kebabs are a fantastic alternative to meatballs, as they are quick, easy and perfect for stuffing into a baguette or pitta. You can also serve them with grilled veggies or a fresh salad on the side.

1. In a large mixing bowl, combine all the ingredients except the olive oil, and stir until you get a sticky meat paste.
2. Place a quarter of the meat mixture on to one half of a sheet of baking paper. Fold the paper over the meat, then use a bench scraper or the edge of a spatula to gently press the mixture into an even log. Cut this into thirds and repeat with the remaining mixture until you end up with 12 logs.
3. Preheat your air fryer to 200°C, then place the cevapi into the air-fryer basket and cook for 10 minutes until crispy and charred on the edges.
4. Stuff them into the ciabattas, dollop over some ajvar, onions and parsley, and serve.

500g beef mince

1 tsp vegetable bouillon powder

1 tsp sweet paprika

½ tsp baking powder (helps to tenderise and keep them juicy)

2–3 tbsp cold sparkling water

1 tbsp olive oil

Salt and black pepper, to taste

SERVE

4 ciabattas, opened (gluten-free if needed)

Ajvar (see Top Tip)

Handful of chopped white onions

Handful of chopped parsley

Top Tip Ajvar is a Balkan condiment, also known as 'Balkan caviar'. It's made from roasted sweet red peppers, and often aubergine, along with garlic and a variety of spices.

You can freeze the cevapi or even make them ahead of time and leave them in the fridge overnight until you are ready to cook them.

SERVES: 4   PREP + COOK TIME: 15 minutes

RAINBOW NOODLES

This recipe is all about ease, colour and big flavours. It makes a refreshing cold meal, which means that once made, you don't have to race to get the kids to the table, they can just help themselves. Rice noodles make it a breeze to throw together, cooking in just minutes. Then it's all about using what you have, so you can grab any leftover veggies from your fridge, chop them up and toss them in. The star of the dish is a sweet and spicy peanut dressing that brings everything together.

250g rice noodles
1 small carrot, thinly sliced
1 red pepper, thinly sliced
100g cucumber, thinly sliced
100g purple cabbage, shredded
3 spring onions, sliced
50g roasted peanuts, roughly chopped
Small handful of coriander, chopped
1 lime, cut into wedges, to serve

SPICY PEANUT DRESSING

3 tbsp peanut butter, smooth or crunchy
1 tbsp soy sauce (or tamari for gluten-free)
1 tbsp lime juice
1 tbsp maple syrup (or honey if non-vegan)
1 tsp chilli flakes
1 small garlic clove, minced
2–3 tbsp warm water

1. Prepare the rice noodles according to the packet instructions, then drain and rinse under cold water to prevent them sticking together.

2. In a small bowl, prepare the dressing by combining all the ingredients and adding enough of the warm water to turn it into a pourable sauce.

3. In a large mixing bowl, toss the noodles with the vegetables and dressing until combined. Sprinkle over the peanuts and coriander, and serve with lime wedges for squeezing.

SERVES: 4   PREP + COOK TIME: 15 minutes

CORNED BEEF ROUGAILLE

This beloved Mauritian dish is pure comfort in a bowl and holds a special place in my heart, especially as it got me through uni! Known by different names around the world, like 'corned beef stew' in West Africa and 'bully beef' in the Caribbean, this Mauritian version is made with tender corned beef cooked in a spicy and tangy tomato sauce. Served with fragrant white rice and chutney, it's a satisfying meal that delivers immediate comfort.

2 tbsp vegetable oil

1 large onion, diced

2 sprigs of thyme

1 tbsp garlic and ginger paste

3 large tomatoes, chopped

½ tsp paprika

1 tbsp tomato paste

340g tin of corned beef, cut into chunks

250ml water

Salt and black pepper, to taste

SERVE

Cooked white rice

Mauritian Chilli Sauce (page 157)

Chopped coriander

1. Heat the oil in a large pan over a high heat. Add the onion and thyme and sauté for 2 minutes until golden.

2. Add the garlic and ginger paste, tomatoes, paprika and tomato paste, and cook for 3–4 minutes.

3. Add the corned beef, breaking it up with a spoon, and stir well to coat in the spiced tomato sauce. Pour in the water, then bring the mixture to a simmer and cook for 10–15 minutes until the sauce thickens. Season with plenty of pepper and a pinch of salt (the corned beef is usually quite salty, so be careful).

4. Serve the rougaille hot over fluffy white rice, with Mauritian chilli sauce on the side and a sprinkling of fresh coriander.

SERVES: 4–6   PREP + COOK TIME: 15 minutes

SMOKY CHICKPEAS WITH SUNDRIED TOMATOES

I love the simplicity of this recipe! It's cooked in less than 15 minutes, making it the perfect dish for those busy days when you want something quick and delicious. The ingredients are easy to find, and the steps are super straightforward. Whether you pair it with couscous or just enjoy it with some crusty bread, this dish is packed with fibre and protein to keep you feeling full.

1. Add the sundried tomatoes and their oil to a pan, along with the garlic. Cook over a medium heat for 1–2 minutes until fragrant.
2. Add the chickpeas, tomatoes, cream and paprika and cook for 5 minutes more, allowing them to heat through.
3. Stir in the lemon zest and juice, and season to taste. Serve sprinkled with coriander or parsley.

100g sundried tomatoes, chopped, oil reserved

3 garlic cloves, minced

2 x 400g tins of chickpeas, drained and rinsed

150g baby plum tomatoes, halved

200ml double cream or vegan cream

1 tsp smoked paprika

Zest and juice of 1 lemon

Salt and pepper, to taste

Coriander or parsley, for garnish

SERVES: 4–6   PREP + COOK TIME: 15 minutes

CHILLI BEEF WITH BROCCOLI

This dish is ridiculously easy and packed with bold flavours, so it's perfect for immediate comfort in a bowl on busy midweek nights. Minced beef is ideal because of its quick cook time, and I find it allows this meal to stretch further than it would if made with sliced beef. However, if you have steak at hand, go ahead and finely slice it against the grain, then cook it in the same way. I serve mine with sticky white rice – this is the kind of comfort food that's best eaten with a spoon!

500g beef mince

1 tbsp vegetable or sesame oil

2 garlic cloves, minced

2.5cm piece of fresh ginger, peeled and grated

1-2 large red chillies (depending on how hot you want it), finely sliced

1 head of broccoli (250g), cut into small florets

2 tbsp water

3 spring onions, sliced

Handful of coriander, chopped

SAUCE

2 tbsp soy sauce (or tamari for gluten-free)

1 tbsp oyster sauce

½ tsp vegetable bouillon powder

1 tbsp honey

1 tsp brown sugar

1 tsp black pepper

2–3 tbsp water

SERVE

Cooked sticky white rice

Crispy chilli oil (optional)

1. In a small bowl, mix together the sauce ingredients, then set aside.

2. Heat a pan over a medium–high heat, then add the beef and cook for 5–7 minutes, breaking it up with a spoon, until browned and releasing its juices. Add the garlic, ginger and red chillies. Cook for another 1–2 minutes until fragrant.

3. Add the broccoli florets and the water, then cover with a lid. This will help the broccoli steam – you want to just take the rawness out, but keep the florets crisp and tender. This should take 3–4 minutes.

4. Pour in the sauce and mix everything well, making sure the beef and broccoli are covered and glossy. Turn off the heat.

5. Sprinkle over the spring onions and chopped coriander. Serve immediately over sticky white rice. You can drizzle over some crispy chilli oil if you want an extra kick, like me!

SERVES: 2 **PREP + COOK TIME: 15 minutes**

KOREAN TOFU JJIGAE

This is ridiculously easy to make, and so comforting. You'd never believe it only takes 15 minutes! The key to this recipe is using a good-quality kimchi, so pick a brand you really love, as it's the heart of this dish. The tofu cooks perfectly in the spicy, flavourful broth, making every bite so satisfying. I usually make just two portions of this, because my nephew isn't a fan of cabbage. When my daughter and I have this, our noses drip and our bellies warm up; it's the perfect dish to heat you from the inside out!

1. In a saucepan, combine the kimchi, vegetable stock, gochujang, gochugaru, soy sauce, sesame oil, onion, garlic and sugar. Bring to the boil and cook for 3–4 minutes, allowing the flavours to come together.
2. Carefully add the sliced tofu to the pan then bring to a simmer and let it warm through and absorb the flavours of the stew for 2–3 minutes.
3. Once everything is heated through and the broth is fragrant, garnish with chopped spring onions and serve hot with white rice. Always eat this with a spoon!

100g kimchi, chopped
200ml vegetable stock
1 tbsp gochujang paste
1 tsp gochugaru (Korean chilli flakes) or chilli flakes
1 tbsp soy sauce (or tamari for gluten-free)
1 tsp sesame oil
¼ onion, sliced
2 garlic cloves, minced
½ tsp sugar
150g silken tofu, cut into large slices

SERVE

2 spring onions, chopped
Cooked white rice

SERVES: 4–6   PREP + COOK TIME: 15 minutes

SAVOURY CABBAGE PANCAKES

Cabbage is one of my secret ingredients when it comes to adding extra veggies without the kids knowing, as it adds a subtle sweetness to curries and stews. In this recipe, however, it finally gets the spotlight! These crispy, chewy pancakes come together in minutes with just a few ingredients. I love topping mine with Japanese mayo, shredded nori sheets and pickled ginger for an extra umami kick!

1. Put the cabbage in a mixing bowl and add the spring onions, rice flour, eggs, water, soy sauce, salt and pepper. Mix thoroughly. You should have a thick, pancake-like batter; if it is too thick, loosen it with a few teaspoons of water until you get the perfect consistency.

2. Heat the oil in a frying pan over a medium heat. Spoon in some of the batter to form a pancake about the size of a small side plate. Cook for 3–4 minutes per side until golden brown and crispy. Transfer to a plate and cover with a clean tea towel to keep warm while you make the rest of the pancakes.

3. Drizzle the pancakes with Japanese mayo and sriracha, sprinkle with shredded nori, and add a few slices of pickled ginger and sesame seeds. Serve immediately and enjoy!

300g white cabbage, finely shredded (see Top Tip)

2 spring onions, finely sliced

100g rice flour

2 medium eggs

50–75ml water

1 tsp soy sauce (or tamari for gluten-free)

Salt and black pepper, to taste

3 tbsp vegetable oil, for shallow-frying

SERVE

Drizzle of Kewpie mayo

Drizzle of sriracha

Shredded nori

Pickled ginger slices

Sprinkling of black sesame seeds

Top Tip To prepare the cabbage, I use a speed peeler, to cut it into long, fine shreds.

COMFORTING
Crowd-pleasers

You know those dishes you can put on the table without a second thought, with no complaints and no last-minute requests for something else? That's what this chapter is all about. Each one is ready within 45 minutes, so you can get a home-cooked meal on the table fast, without stress. They're the dishes that wrap you up like a hug, fill small and big bellies alike, and bring that little sense of accomplishment on those long hump days. No fuss, quick to make, and even quicker to disappear!

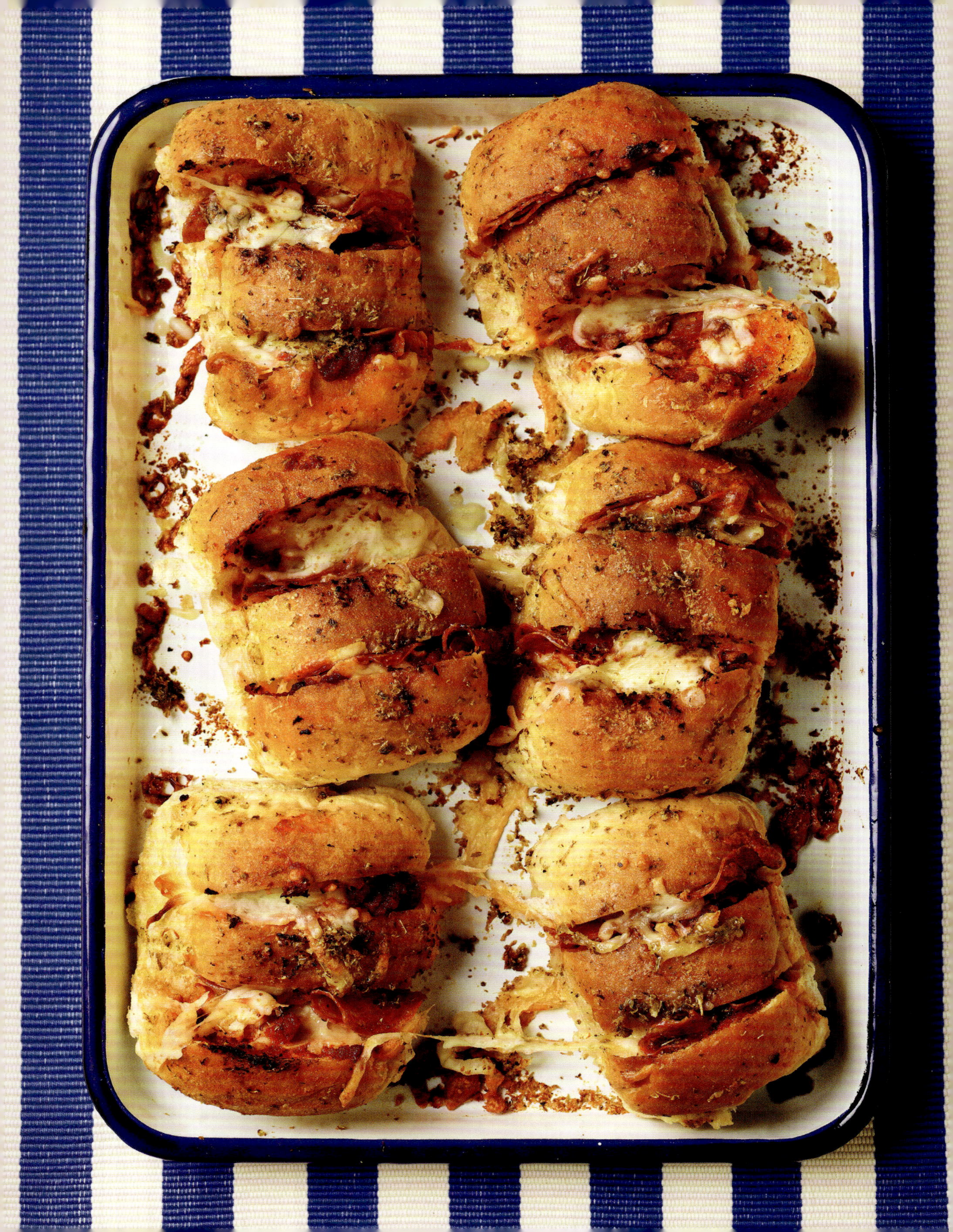

SERVES: 4–6 **PREP + COOK TIME: 20 minutes**

PULL-APART PIZZA ROLLS

Occasionally, my daughter will have a midweek playdate, usually when I'm helping out another family, and on those days, this is what I will make. I tend to keep bread rolls in the freezer, but I don't often stock pizza or pre-made items. I've realised that I'm more of an 'ingredients household', so this is a quick way to have all the flavours of a pizza without having to call in for one. I've found that kids absolutely love these rolls because they're so simple to make and fun to eat; you just pull them apart and enjoy.

1. Preheat your oven to 160°C fan/180°C/350°F.
2. In a bowl, combine the tomato paste with the olive oil and mix well.
3. Make two vertical cuts in each roll, making sure you don't cut all the way through – about two-thirds of the way is perfect. Brush in some of the tomato paste/oil. After you have filled all the holes with the tomato mixture, you can stuff each one with a piece of pepperoni and some mozzarella.
4. In a small bowl, combine the garlic granules, oregano and melted butter, then brush this mixture over the rolls. Bake in the oven for 12–15 minutes until they are golden on top and the cheese is melted and bubbly.
5. Serve warm and enjoy!

6 soft rolls

2 tbsp Turkish tomato paste

2 tbsp olive oil

12 pieces of pepperoni (we use halal beef/turkey pepperoni)

100g mozzarella, grated

1 tsp garlic granules

1 tbsp dried oregano

100g butter, melted

SERVES: 4–6　　　　　　　　　　　　　　　PREP + COOK TIME: 35 minutes

AIR-FRIED CHICKEN

There's nothing worse than dealing with the greasy mess after frying chicken, when the hob has been splattered with oil and there's a pile of dishes to wash up! We love fried chicken at home, but this method gives you all the crunch, flavour and comfort of the classic, without the hassle. Crispy, golden and air-fried to perfection, this is the easy way to enjoy fried chicken any night of the week. You will be amazed by my iced-water hack, which means you don't have to make a special trip to the shop for buttermilk!

150g plain flour

50g cornflour

1 tsp baking powder (helps with crispiness)

1 tsp vegetable bouillon powder

½ tsp salt

1 tsp ground black pepper

1 tbsp smoked paprika

1 tbsp garlic granules

1 tbsp onion powder

1 tsp cayenne pepper

2 medium eggs

500ml water with ice cubes

6–8 boneless chicken thighs, skin on

Avocado oil spray

1. Preheat the air fryer to 200°C and line the basket with baking paper.

2. In a large bowl, mix together the flours, baking powder, bouillon powder, salt, pepper and spices. In a separate bowl, whisk the eggs. Add the water and ice cubes to a third bowl.

3. Dip a chicken thigh first into the egg mixture, then the spiced flour mixture, shaking off any excess flour. Now dip it into the ice-cold water, then back into the spiced flour. Repeat the process for all the chicken thighs, then add the coated chicken to the air fryer and spray them all with avocado oil to help them crisp up.

4. Air-fry for 25 minutes, turning halfway through and spraying with more oil until golden brown and cooked through.

5. Serve hot with your favourite dips, slaw or a side of fries.

Top Tip You need to be generous with the avocado oil, and coat the chicken all over to create that wonderful crunch.

SERVES: 4 **PREP + COOK TIME: 20 minutes**

PRAWN AND PLANTAIN CURRY

I'm not normally inspired by hotel menus, but this dish is different. I had it at The Sandpiper Hotel in Barbados during the annual food festival, and after a long-haul flight and a dose of jet lag, it was exactly what I needed. A rich, spiced coconut sauce, the sweetness of perfectly cooked plantains, and tender, juicy prawns made every bite feel like sunshine on a plate. Whenever I make it at home, it instantly takes me back to those warm Bajan evenings and puts a massive smile on my face. Served with a heap of white rice and some steamed cabbage on the side, one taste of this iconic Bajan yellow hot pepper sauce and I'm all good – the stress of the day is forgotten.

1. Heat the oil in a large pan over a high heat. Add the spring onions, along with some salt, and cook for 2–3 minutes until softened.

2. Stir in the garlic and ginger paste, curry powder and ground allspice. Cook for another minute until fragrant, then add the red pepper, plantains and coconut milk, and cook for 10 minutes until the plantains are tender.

3. Add the prawns and cook for a few minutes more until they turn pink and are just cooked, then turn off the heat and allow the prawns to finish cooking in the residual heat of the pan. This helps you to avoid overcooking them.

4. Stir in the lime juice and season with salt and pepper to taste. Serve hot, garnished with spring onions and fresh coriander.

1 tbsp vegetable oil

4 spring onions, sliced, plus extra for garnish

1 tbsp garlic and ginger paste

2 tbsp West Indian/Caribbean curry powder, or mild masala

½ tsp ground allspice

1 red pepper, sliced

2 ripe plantains, peeled and sliced into rounds

400ml tin of full-fat coconut milk

200g raw prawns, peeled and cleaned

Juice of 1 lime

Salt and black pepper, to taste

Chopped coriander, to garnish

SERVES: 6–8

PREP + COOK TIME: 25 minutes

MOROCCAN VEGETABLE TAGINE

On my most recent trip to Morocco, I had the pleasure of being taught to cook this dish by the inspiration that is Alia Al Kasimi from Cooking with Alia. I've watched her for years, so to finally cook alongside her was such a pleasure. This is a recipe I'm excited to pass down to Niyyah, and now I get to share it with you! Filled with a delicious blend of spices and hearty ingredients like potatoes, carrots, cabbage and chickpeas, this tagine is naturally vegan and gluten-free, full of rich flavours and perfect for a cosy, wholesome meal.

1. Heat the olive oil in a large saucepan over a medium heat. Add the onion and sauté for a few minutes until softened, then add the garlic, salt and pepper and spices and cook for another minute until fragrant.

2. Add the vegetable stock, potatoes, carrots, cabbage and preserved lemon to the pot and bring to the boil. Cover and reduce the heat to a simmer for 15–20 minutes, until the vegetables are tender, then add the chickpeas and cook for a few minutes more.

3. Serve the tagine hot (here's where you can take out the decorative tagine you bought on that trip!) and stack the vegetables in a cone shape: I usually add more cabbage to the bottom of the dish to create a base, and then follow with the carrots and potatoes. Sprinkle over the remaining chickpeas and sauce to finish. Garnish with fresh coriander and lemon wedges on the side and use the bread to mop up all the juices.

2 tbsp olive oil

1 large onion, grated

2 garlic cloves finely grated

1 tbsp ground cumin

1 tsp ground coriander

1 tsp ground cinnamon

¼ tsp ground turmeric

½ tsp ground ginger

550ml vegetable stock

1 tsp paprika

2 potatoes, peeled and cut into large wedges

3 carrots, peeled and halved

½ small cabbage, cut into 8

1 preserved lemon, cut into 8

400g tin of chickpeas, drained and rinsed

Salt and black pepper, to taste

SERVE

Handful of chopped coriander

Lemon wedges

Fresh baguette or khobz (or gluten-free alternatives)

SERVES: 4–6   PREP + COOK TIME: 45 minutes

CHICKEN PERI PERI TRAYBAKE

Nando's-style rice is always a winner, and this version is made all in one tray. Spicy red rice topped with flavour-packed wings, baked until perfect in the oven: it's a fuss-free dish with very little washing-up, as we love to dig straight in from the same dish, with everyone choosing their own section to eat from! Perfect for a midweek meal that's comforting and full of flavour, but more importantly, easy.

6 chicken wings, skin on

2 tbsp peri peri seasoning

300g basmati rice (I use golden sella basmati, grand extra-long or easy-cook), rinsed

1 tbsp smoked paprika

1 tbsp garlic granules

3 tbsp Turkish tomato paste

500ml vegetable stock

½ red pepper, sliced

½ yellow pepper, sliced

SERVE

Handful of chopped coriander

1 lemon, cut into wedges

1. Preheat the oven to 180°C fan/200°C/400°F. Separate the wings into drumettes and flats to make 12 pieces in total. In a large bowl, coat the chicken pieces with the peri peri seasoning and set aside.

2. In a large ovenproof saucepan, combine the rice, spices, tomato paste and vegetable stock, mixing it all together until the rice is a vibrant red.

3. Arrange the chicken wings on top of the rice in a circle, then cover the pan with a lid and cook over a high heat for 5 minutes. Reduce the heat to low and simmer for another 15 minutes.

4. Remove the lid and sprinkle over the pepper slices, then transfer to the oven and cook for another 10–15 minutes, uncovered, to allow the wings to get crispy.

5. Scatter with fresh coriander and serve with lemon wedges, getting stuck in straight from the dish Enjoy!

SERVES: 4–6
PREP + COOK TIME: 20 minutes

PRAWN BUTTER MASALA

Juicy prawns simmered in a rich, buttery tomato sauce infused with warming spices: this dish is pure comfort food. It's made even easier with frozen onions and garlic and ginger paste, so you can have what feels like a take-away on the table in no time. Perfect with naan or rice – and I love to have a dollop of yoghurt, plus some salad and mango pickle on the side.

1. Heat the butter and oil in a saucepan over a high heat. Add the onions, along with some salt, and cook for 3–4 minutes until softened and translucent.
2. Add the garlic and ginger paste, curry powder and all the spices, toasting the spices for 1–2 minutes, until fragrant.
3. Add the passata, sugar and tomato paste and season with salt. Reduce the heat to medium and cook for another 10 minutes – keep stirring, and bear in mind that this will spit at you, so use the lid as your guard!
4. Add the double cream and prawns and cook for 3 minutes more, until the prawns have turned pink and are just cooked. They will continue to cook in the residual heat of the pan. Stir in the kasuri methi.
5. Serve hot, garnished with fresh coriander.

1 tbsp butter
1 tbsp vegetable oil
100g frozen chopped onions
1 tbsp garlic and ginger paste
2 tbsp medium curry powder
1 tsp garam masala
1 tsp Kashmiri chilli powder
400g jar passata
1 tsp white caster sugar
2 tbsp Turkish tomato paste
100ml double cream
350g raw prawns, peeled and deveined
1 tsp kasuri methi (dried fenugreek leaves), crushed between the palms of your hands
Salt, to taste
Chopped coriander, to serve

SERVES: 4–6   PREP + COOK TIME: 45 minutes

SATURDAY SOUP WITH DUMPLINGS

This is a hearty, rich Jamaican favourite that's usually reserved for Saturdays. Normally made with chicken, this vegan version, packed with cassava, sweetcorn and chewy dumplings, gives you quick comfort and will still warm your soul and satisfy those cravings, even though it's made in just 45 minutes. Using frozen, pre-chopped cassava makes it even easier to put together. Perfect for those days when you feel you have the sniffles coming on, or the household just needs the perfect pick-me-up.

2 tbsp vegetable oil
50g frozen chopped onions
½ tsp ground turmeric
2 garlic cloves, minced
Sprig of thyme
1 tbsp all-purpose seasoning
1 tsp vegetable bouillon powder
1 tsp allspice berries
2 carrots, chopped
300g frozen chopped cassava
2 corn on the cob, each cut into 3 pieces
400ml tin of full-fat coconut milk
1.2 litres vegetable stock
2 spring onions, whole
1 Scotch bonnet chilli, whole
Salt, to taste

DUMPLINGS

150g plain flour
½ tsp salt
80ml warm water

1. Heat the oil in a large pot over a high heat and add the onions, turmeric, garlic, thyme, all-purpose seasoning, bouillon powder and allspice berries. Cook for 2–3 minutes until fragrant.

2. Add the vegetables, coconut milk and vegetable stock, along with the spring onions and Scotch bonnet (pierce it to bring out the flavour). Bring to the boil, then reduce the heat to medium, cover and cook for 15 minutes.

3. Meanwhile, make the dumplings by combining the flour and salt in a bowl. Gradually add the water, kneading until a soft, sticky dough forms. Pinch off small pieces and roll them into oval logs around 5cm long. Drop these directly into the soup.

4. Cook with the lid on for a further 10 minutes until the dumplings are cooked through and the soup is rich and flavourful. Taste for seasoning and adjust as needed. Remove the Scotch bonnet and serve the soup hot.

SERVES: 4   **PREP + COOK TIME: 15 minutes**

UDON AND DUMPLING RAMEN

This is the kind of meal that saves the day when you're tired and hungry and need something warm, satisfying and ridiculously easy. Thick, chewy udon noodles, juicy dumplings and a flavour-packed broth come together in minutes, all thanks to a well-stocked freezer. The only reason I don't make this as regularly as I'd like is because dumplings can be expensive, and we are definitely an 'ingredients house'.
But you can easily make this style of noodle dish without the dumplings; just add extra vegetables to bulk it out.

1 litre hot chicken stock

2 tbsp soy sauce

1 tbsp miso paste

1 tsp sesame oil

2 garlic cloves, minced

1 tsp grated ginger

12 frozen dumplings (any variety)

2 packs (400g total) fresh or frozen udon noodles

2 pak choi, quartered

GARNISH

2 spring onions, finely sliced

Sesame seeds

Crispy chilli oil (optional)

1. In a large pot over a high heat, combine the hot stock with the soy sauce, miso paste, sesame oil, garlic and ginger. Stir well until the miso paste dissolves. Bring to the boil and add the frozen dumplings, then cook for 3 minutes.

2. Add the udon noodles and pak choi and cook for another 2 minutes if using fresh noodles, or 4 minutes if using frozen.

3. Divide the udon noodles and dumplings between four bowls, then ladle over the stock and pak choi.

4. Top with sliced spring onions and sesame seeds and serve. You can add extra heat with some crispy chilli oil, if desired.

SERVES: 6   PREP + COOK TIME: 20 minutes

MOROCCAN HARIRA

We always call this Ramadan soup, because it's on the table every single evening during that month! My daughter is half Moroccan, so this dish isn't just a meal, it's part of her heritage. Harira is a comforting, rich soup, packed with lentils, chickpeas and vermicelli, gently thickened with flour or cornflour, and always finished with cumin and a squeeze of fresh lemon. It's nourishing, deeply satisfying and full of warmth, perfect for filling a gap after those long, tiring fasting days. You can make up a batch and keep it in the freezer.

2 tbsp olive oil

1 onion, grated

1 tsp ground ginger

1 tsp ground turmeric

1 tsp ground cinnamon

1 tsp ground cumin, plus extra to serve

1 tsp sweet paprika

2 tbsp Turkish tomato paste

1.2 litres vegetable stock

½ x 400g tin of chickpeas, drained and rinsed

400g cooked brown lentils

2 tbsp cornflour

50g vermicelli pasta (or broken spaghetti)

Juice of ½ lemon, plus wedges to serve

Handful of coriander and parsley, finely chopped

Salt and black pepper, to taste

Extra virgin olive oil, to serve

1. Heat the olive oil in a large pot over a high heat. Add the onion, spices and tomato paste, and cook for 3–4 minutes until fragrant.

2. Add most of the stock, reserving 100ml, along with the chickpeas and lentils. Bring to the boil.

3. Combine the cornflour and the reserved stock to form a paste, then stir this into the pan, mixing well to avoid lumps. Toss in the vermicelli and cook for a few minutes until the pasta is completely cooked.

4. Season with salt and black pepper, then stir in the lemon juice and chopped herbs. Ladle into soup bowls and serve with a pinch of cumin and a drizzle of extra virgin olive oil.

SERVES: 4   PREP + COOK TIME: 20 minutes

MAURITIAN CARROT AND RED LENTIL SOUP

This comforting and hearty soup is a true Mauritian favourite. To help speed things up in the kitchen, I'm using pre-cooked lentils, but you can also opt for the traditional method and use dried lentils, making it in a pressure cooker to cut the cooking time. This nourishing soup is rich and silky, perfect for warming you up on chilly days. It's simple to prepare, full of flavour and packed with wholesome, protein-rich ingredients.

1. Heat the oil in a large pot over a medium heat. Add the onion, garlic and ginger paste, cumin seeds and thyme, sautéing for 3–5 minutes until softened and fragrant.
2. Stir in the tomatoes, carrots, lentils and stock. Bring to the boil, then reduce the heat to a simmer. Cook for 10 minutes until the carrots are just tender.
3. Season with salt and pepper to taste. Serve hot, garnished with fresh coriander, with a baguette on the side, if you like.

- 2 tbsp neutral oil
- 1 large onion, diced
- 1 tbsp garlic and ginger paste
- 1 tsp cumin seeds
- 2 sprigs of thyme
- 2 tomatoes, finely chopped
- 4 carrots, peeled and chopped
- 400g tin of lentils in water, drained
- 1.5 litres vegetable or chicken stock
- Salt and black pepper, to taste
- Chopped coriander, to garnish
- Crusty baguette, to serve (optional)

Top Tip Have with some baguette (or gluten-free bread) on the side, if you like.

SERVES: 4   PREP + COOK TIME: 20 minutes

'MARRY ME' SALMON

Most of the time, Marry Me Chicken is the go-to for date night, but why can't we switch it up and enjoy Marry Me Salmon? This creamy salmon fillet in a rich, flavourful sauce is perfect for a midweek pick-me-up. It's quick, comforting, and still packed with all the indulgence you need to treat yourself after a busy day. I love pairing mine with Batata Harra (see page 167) and Garlicky Lemon Broccoli (see page 154) for the perfect meal!

1. Coat the salmon fillets with the oil, garlic granules, oregano, chilli flakes and salt and pepper, then sear in a frying pan over a high heat for 2 minutes on each side. Once cooked, remove the salmon from the pan and set aside on a plate.

2. Using the same pan, make the sauce. Sauté the sundried tomatoes in their oil, along with the garlic, for 2 minutes until fragrant.

3. Add the cream, stock, lemon zest and juice and oregano. Season to taste, then bring the mixture to a gentle bubble.

4. Return the salmon to the pan and let it warm through in the sauce for around 3 minutes, until fully cooked. To serve, sprinkle over some Parmesan cheese and garnish with fresh parsley.

4 salmon fillets, skin on, butterflied (see Top Tip)
1 tbsp olive oil
1 tsp garlic granules
1 tsp dried oregano
½ tsp chilli flakes
Pinch of salt and black pepper

'MARRY ME' SAUCE
6 sundried tomatoes from a jar and their oil, chopped
3 garlic cloves, minced
200ml double cream
200ml chicken stock
Zest and juice of ½ lemon
1 tsp dried oregano

GARNISH
30g Parmesan, grated
Chopped parsley

Top Tip To 'butterfly' the salmon, just slice it down the centre horizontally to create two fillets.

SERVES: 6–8

PREP + COOK TIME: 15 minutes

BLACKENED SALMON TACOS WITH MANGO SALSA

With this recipe, we often make the salmon then shred it into tacos. It really helps to stretch the meal, especially when you are on a budget and have a few extra guests popping in. It's a fun and interactive way to eat, and I've found that when we have this on the table, the kids are so busy filling their tacos they end up talking more. It's the best time to ask if they got into any trouble at school that day – you'll be surprised what comes out when they're focused on their food!

1. In a large bowl, combine the oil, smoked paprika, cumin, garlic granules and thyme, along with salt and pepper. Add the salmon and, using your hands, rub this paste generously over both sides of the fillets.

2. Spray the oil into a large frying pan over a high heat. Once hot, place the salmon fillets into the pan and cook for about 3 minutes on each side, or until the salmon is blackened on the outside and cooked through.

3. Meanwhile, in a small bowl, combine the salsa ingredients.

4. Place the cooked salmon fillets on plates and top with the fresh mango salsa. Serve with fresh coriander, lime wedges, tacos and hot sauce, and let everyone serve themselves.

2 tbsp olive oil

2 tbsp smoked paprika

1 tbsp ground cumin

1 tbsp garlic granules

½ tsp dried thyme

4 salmon fillets, skin on, butterflied (see Top Tip)

Avocado oil spray

Salt and pepper, to taste

SALSA

1 ripe mango, peeled and diced

¼ red onion, finely chopped

1 small red chili, finely chopped

Juice of 1 lime, plus wedges to serve

SERVE

Chopped coriander

Soft tacos

Hot sauce

Top Tip To 'butterfly' the salmon, just slice it down the centre horizontally to create two fillets.

SERVES: 6–8　　　　　　　　　　　　　　　　　　　PREP + COOK TIME: 40 minutes

MAURITIAN MOULOUKTANI CHICKEN

On a recent trip to Mauritius, I was taught how to make this traditional Mauritian favourite, by Chef Ravi. He shared a sweet memory of how his mother used to make it as a way of serving lots of kids, and it's a great reminder of how to make meals stretch, especially when served with rice or bread. The dish combines tender chicken pieces with yellow split peas, cooked together in a savoury broth with light spices that bring out a subtle yet delicious flavour. For speed, I'm using mung daal instead of yellow split peas here.

2 tbsp vegetable oil

1kg whole chicken, cut into pieces, bone in, skin on

½ tsp ground turmeric

1 tsp ground cumin

50g frozen chopped onions

1 tbsp garlic and ginger paste

1–2 small dried chillies

6 curry leaves (or 1 bay leaf)

1 tsp garam masala

100g mung daal

1.5 litres chicken stock (I use stock cubes)

Salt, to taste

Chopped mint, to garnish

1. Heat the oil in a large pot over a medium heat. Add the chicken pieces, along with the turmeric and cumin, and fry for around 3 minutes, until browned. Remove from the pan and set aside.

2. Using the same pan, sauté the onions for 2 minutes until softened, then stir in the garlic and ginger paste, chillies, curry leaves and garam masala. Cook for another 1–2 minutes until fragrant.

3. Return the chicken pieces to the pot, along with the mung daal and stock. Bring to the boil and cook for 20–30 minutes, stirring occasionally and checking to see if the daal is cooked.

4. Adjust the seasoning, then serve hot, garnished with finely chopped mint.

SERVES: 4–6   PREP + COOK TIME: 30 minutes

DOMODA – PEANUT STEW WITH OKRA AND SWEET POTATO

My friend Abie has always made the best peanut stew, hands down. She's from Gambia, and her version of Domoda, the national dish of her home country, is rich, comforting and packed with bold flavours. This hearty dish brings together sweet potatoes, chickpeas and a creamy peanut butter base for the ultimate plant-based comfort food. It's quick to make, full of warmth and guaranteed to leave you scraping the bowl for more.

1. In a small blender, blend the onion, spring onions, Scotch bonnet, garlic paste and tomato paste.
2. Heat the oil in a large saucepan over a high heat and add the blended mixture, cooking for around 10 minutes until it begins to split and the oil comes to the surface.
3. In a jug, combine the peanut butter with the hot stock, stirring until smooth. Add this to the pan, along with the bouillon powder and all-purpose seasoning. Season with salt and bring to the boil, then add the sweet potato, carrots and chickpeas, and cook for 10 minutes more.
4. Add the baby okra and season with salt again, if needed, then cook for a final 5 minutes.
5. Serve with white rice.

1 onion, quartered

3 spring onions, roughly chopped

½ Scotch bonnet chilli

1 tbsp garlic paste

3 tbsp Turkish tomato paste

3–4 tbsp vegetable oil

80g smooth peanut butter

600ml hot vegetable stock

1 tsp vegetable bouillon powder

1 tsp all-purpose seasoning

1 large sweet potato, peeled and diced

3 carrots, peeled and cut into thirds

400g tin of chickpeas, drained and rinsed

150g frozen whole baby okra

Salt, to taste

Cooked white rice, to serve

SERVES: 6–8   PREP + COOK TIME: 35 minutes

AIR-FRYER KEBABS

Instead of heading out for take-away on a Friday night, you can create delicious, restaurant-quality kebabs at home! The secret is rolling the spiced minced meat into a log, wrapping it in foil and cooking it in the air fryer. When I posted this video on my Instagram, it went viral within 5 hours! This method locks in the flavour and juiciness of the meat and mimics a doner, where you slice the kebabs thinly after cooking.

500g lamb or beef mince (or a mix of both – just make sure it is a fatty mix)

1 tbsp ground cumin

1 tsp garlic granules

1 tbsp ground paprika

1 tsp ground coriander

½ tsp ground cinnamon

1 tsp ground black pepper

¼ tsp salt

1 tbsp vegetable bouillon powder

1–2 tbsp chopped parsley and coriander

SERVE

Your favourite pickled veggies

Fresh flatbreads or pita (optional)

Tahini sauce or Garlic yoghurt (optional, see page 135)

1. In a large bowl, mix the meat, spices, seasoning, bouillon powder and chopped herbs until well combined.

2. Shape the meat mixture into a log or sausage shape, pressing it tightly together so it holds. Wrap in tin foil, ensuring it's completely sealed.

3. Preheat the air fryer to 180°C. Place the foil-wrapped kebab into the air-fryer basket and cook for 20–25 minutes, turning halfway through. Once cooked, remove from the air fryer and allow the kebab to rest for a few minutes before unwrapping the foil. It should be cooked through and have a nice golden-brown colour on the outside.

4. Slice the kebab into long, thin pieces, slicing along the length rather than cutting it into circles.

5. Serve with pickled veggies and warm flatbreads or pita. You can also drizzle the kebabs with some tahini sauce or my Garlic Yoghurt, if you like.

SERVES: 4–6 PREP + COOK TIME: 25 minutes

FIVE-INGREDIENT COCONUT CHICKEN CURRY

This is cooked on rotation at least once a week at my house. This was one of my very first viral videos on TikTok – partly because it was so simple, but mainly because people complained that I dunked my whole hand into the pot with a roti. I mean, it was cooked for my family! Once I realised that I could cook a curry like this and it would taste so delicious, I reserved 'proper' curry cooking for the weekend, when I have time to labour over cutting the onions and chopping fresh garlic and ginger. None of that is needed here! Customise by adding chutney, fresh coriander or chilli on top, for anyone who wants it, and serve with steamed rice, naan or roti.

1. Heat the oil in a pot over a medium–high heat. Add the chicken and sear for 5 minutes to give it some colour and render down any fat.

2. After 5 minutes, push the chicken to the edges of the pan and add the tomato paste, curry powder and a quarter of the coconut milk. Set aside a small amount of coconut milk for garnishing. Stir to create a thick paste. Cook this down for a few minutes to cook off the spices and get as much flavour as you can into your curry.

3. Now pour in the rest of the coconut milk, then half-fill the tin with water and pour that in too. Crumble in the chicken stock cube and stir everything together.

4. Cover the pot with a lid and cook for a further 10–15 minutes until the sauce has thickened and the chicken is cooked through. Garnish with a drizzle of coconut milk and a few sprigs of coriander and serve.

1 tbsp olive oil

600g boneless and skinless chicken thighs, cut into 3cm chunks

3 tbsp Turkish tomato paste

3 tbsp curry powder (see Top Tip)

400ml tin of full-fat coconut milk

1 chicken stock cube

GARNISH

Coriander

Top Tip In terms of curry powder, I would suggest you opt for a mild madras or mild Caribbean curry powder. If you do want heat, you could choose a hot or medium curry powder, which has chilli running through it.

EVERYDAY *Heroes*

This chapter is all about the recipes you can count on as your midweek lifesavers, your Monday-to-Friday go-to recipes, the meals that never let you down. We all have those days when creativity in the kitchen runs dry, and that's where these dishes step in. They're quick, delicious and easy to pull together, no matter how busy life gets.

I always say that when you buy a cookbook, you flip through it at first, bookmarking the recipes that catch your eye. But over time, there are always those few pages that become worn, oil-splattered and stained: the recipes you come back to time and time again. That's exactly what I want this section to be for you!

SERVES: 4–6 **PREP + COOK TIME: 25 minutes**

SPAGHETTI BOLOGNESE

When I asked my full-time-working mum friends to name a go-to midweek meal that never gets complaints from the kids, their answer was unanimous: spaghetti Bolognese. Most of my friends make it the traditional way, but I had to find a way to speed things up. The ultimate hack? Buying Turkish tomato paste, which is packed with real tomatoes. This adds so much richness and flavour to the sauce, and it means the kids will happily scoff it down. It's honestly the most reliable midweek meal – everyone is happy when this is on the table.

1. Heat the oil in a large saucepan over high heat. Add the beef mince and cook until browned, breaking it apart with a spoon. Add the onions and garlic, along with a heavy pinch of salt, and cook for another few minutes until the onions start to soften and the garlic releases its aroma.

2. Add the tomato paste, sugar and herbs, then cook for 5 minutes more to get all the flavour out of the tomato paste.

3. Pour in the red wine and stir, scraping any bits stuck to the pan, then add the beef stock. Season with some salt and pepper and simmer the sauce for a further 10 minutes.

4. Meanwhile, cook the spaghetti in a pan of boiling water until al dente, according to the packet instructions. Drain, reserving some of the cooking water.

5. Loosen the sauce with some of the reserved pasta water to get the consistency you like, then toss in the cooked spaghetti or serve the sauce on top of the cooked pasta. Garnish with grated Parmesan, chopped parsley and basil.

1 tbsp olive oil

500g beef mince

50g frozen chopped onions

6 garlic cloves, finely grated

4 tbsp Turkish tomato paste

1 tbsp white caster sugar

1 tbsp dried oregano

1 bay leaf

100ml red wine (I use 0% Shiraz)

400ml beef stock

350g dried spaghetti

Salt and black pepper, to taste

SERVE

Plenty of grated Parmesan

Chopped parsley and basil

SERVES: 4 **PREP + COOK TIME: 15 minutes**

NASI GORENG

GF

A staple in Indonesia, nasi goreng is the ultimate quick and satisfying meal, perfect for busy families. It's a brilliant way to use up leftover rice (because, as the saying goes, there's always rice at home!). The secret to its rich, slightly sweet and savoury flavour is kecap manis, which is a thick, caramelised Indonesian soy sauce. Topped with a crispy fried egg and fresh spring onions, this dish is real comfort food and comes together in minutes.

1. Heat the oil in a large frying pan or wok over a high heat. Add the garlic, onion and chilli (if using), along with the chicken, prawns or tofu, and cook for 2–4 minutes until fragrant.
2. Stir in the rice, breaking up any clumps. Add the kecap manis, soy sauce and white pepper. Stir-fry for 3–4 minutes more until everything is well coated.
3. Meanwhile, fry the eggs in oil in a separate frying pan over a medium–high heat for 2–3 minutes, until crispy around the edges. I cook mine sunny side up to achieve the perfectly runny yolk.
4. Serve the rice hot, topped with the fried eggs, spring onions and crispy shallots. If you like, add some cucumber slices for freshness.

2 tbsp vegetable oil (or other neutral oil)

3 garlic cloves, minced

1 small onion, diced

1 red chilli, sliced (optional)

200g chicken, prawns or tofu, diced

600g leftover cooked rice

3 tbsp kecap manis (Indonesian sweet soy sauce, check the label for gluten-free)

1 tbsp soy sauce (or tamari for gluten-free)

½ tsp ground white pepper

4 eggs

SERVE

2 spring onions, sliced

Fried shallots

Cucumber slices (optional)

SERVES: 4 **PREP + COOK TIME: 10 minutes**

CHEESY MICROWAVE MAC MAGIC

Macaroni cheese in the microwave? Yes, you heard that right! This is the ultimate fuss-free, no-brainer meal that needs to be in your midweek dinner rotation. Just throw everything into a bowl, let the microwave do its thing, and – boom! Creamy, cheesy comfort food in minutes. I love serving this with steamed broccoli or even a grilled chicken thigh on the side, but honestly, it's delicious just as it is. My daughter and her friends are huge fans, so trust me, this one's an all-round winner! I like to serve this with my Garlicky Lemon Broccoli (page 156).

- 300g dried macaroni
- 500ml water
- ½ tsp salt
- 250ml whole milk
- 200g grated Cheddar and mozzarella mix
- 1 tsp Dijon mustard (optional)
- 1 tsp garlic granules
- ½ tsp ground black pepper
- 1 heaped tbsp butter
- 3 tbsp grated Parmesan, plus extra to serve

SERVE
- Small pinch of ground nutmeg

1. In a large microwave-safe bowl, combine the macaroni, water and salt. Microwave on High for 5 minutes. If the water isn't fully absorbed by the pasta at this point, cook for another 1–2 minutes on High until the pasta is tender.

2. Add the milk, grated Cheddar and mozzarella, Dijon mustard (if using), garlic granules and black pepper, then stir everything together. Microwave on High for 2 minutes, stirring halfway, until the cheese is melted and the sauce is creamy.

3. Stir in the butter, Parmesan and nutmeg – the more you stir, the more you agitate the starch, which creates a silkier, creamier sauce. Serve immediately topped with extra grated Parmesan.

SERVES: 6–8 PREP + COOK TIME: 30 minutes

CHICKEN SHAWARMA

This tender, spiced chicken shawarma is a weeknight winner, delivering Middle Eastern flavours with minimal effort. Marinated to perfection and all cooked on a baking tray in the oven, this dish is ready in under 30 minutes – no stress! All you need to do is wrap the juicy chicken in warm flatbreads with fresh veggies and serve with a creamy garlic yoghurt sauce. This dish is packed with protein, making it a favourite of my nephew, who's all about the gym – he usually eats three servings of this just to himself!

1. Preheat the oven to 200°C fan/220°C/425°F.
2. Coat the chicken with the oil, garlic, spices, lemon juice and bouillon powder, then spread out the chicken pieces in a single layer on a large baking tray. Roast in the oven for 15 minutes, flipping halfway through, until the chicken is cooked through and golden and crispy in parts.
3. Make the sauce by mixing together the yoghurt, garlic and lemon juice in a bowl, then season with salt and pepper.
4. Serve the chicken in flatbreads with your favourite salad ingredients, with the garlic yoghurt sauce drizzled over the top.

1.2kg boneless, skinless chicken thighs, thinly sliced

2 tbsp olive oil

4 garlic cloves, minced

2 tbsp ground cumin

1 tbsp ground paprika

1 tsp ground coriander

1 tsp ground turmeric

1 tsp ground cinnamon

1 tsp ground allspice

1 tsp ground black pepper

Juice of ½ lemon

1 tsp vegetable bouillon powder

Salt and ground black pepper, to taste

GARLIC YOGHURT SAUCE

200g Greek yoghurt

2 garlic cloves, finely grated, or 1 tsp garlic granules

Juice of ½ lemon

SERVE

6–8 flatbreads (gluten-free if needed)

Cucumbers, tomatoes, red onion and lettuce

SERVES: 4   PREP + COOK TIME: 15 minutes

THAI COCONUT CURRY NOODLE SOUP

This is very loosely based on Khao Soi, a meal I fell in love with when I was in Chiang Mai. It is rich, fragrant and comforting. You can use whatever protein you like – chicken, prawns – or tofu – or just use your favourite mixed veg. Served over egg or rice noodles, it's a bowl of pure comfort.

400ml tin of full-fat coconut milk

1 tbsp garlic and ginger paste

1 tbsp lemongrass paste

2 tbsp mild masala curry powder

400ml chicken or vegetable stock

1 tbsp fish sauce (or vegan fish sauce)

1 tbsp light soy sauce

1 tsp light brown sugar or palm sugar

200g cooked chicken, prawns, tofu or a selection of mixed vegetables

Juice of ½ lime

2 pak choi, halved

300g cooked egg noodles or rice noodles (or use a ready-made packet)

Salt and black pepper, to taste

SERVE

Chopped coriander

Sliced red chilli

Lime wedges

1. Scoop 2 tablespoons of the liquid at the top of the tin of coconut milk, and heat this in a large pan over a medium heat. Add the garlic and ginger paste, lemongrass paste and curry powder, and cook for 2–3 minutes until fragrant.

2. Pour in the rest of the coconut milk, along with the stock, then stir in the fish sauce, soy sauce and sugar. Bring to the boil. Add the pre-cooked chicken, prawns, tofu or mixed veggies for no more than 3 minutes, to ensure everything is heated through. Squeeze in the lime juice and check the seasoning – you can add more salt, sugar or lime, depending on the balance of flavours you want.

3. Add the pak choi and cover the pan with the lid, allowing the leaves to steam for 1 minute until wilted.

4. Divide the noodles between individual serving bowls, then ladle the hot soup over the top. Finish with fresh coriander and red chilli, and serve with lime wedges for squeezing.

Top Tip I often add some fish sauce and sugar to the table so that each person can season their soup as they like.

SERVES: 4   PREP + COOK TIME: 15 minutes

BROWN STEW SALMON

GF

This delicious, Jamaican-inspired salmon dish gets its name from the traditional 'browning' technique that's used to make it, where meats or fish are caramelised to create a deep, rich flavour. In this recipe, I've cheated by using ready-made browning to speed things up, but it still results in a stew that has a beautiful balance of savoury, spicy and rich flavours.

4 salmon fillets, with or without skin, as preferred (see Top Tip)

1 tbsp all-purpose seasoning

1 tbsp vegetable oil

1 large onion, sliced

2 garlic cloves, finely chopped

1 Scotch bonnet chilli, sliced

3 sprigs of thyme

1 tsp allspice berries

½ yellow pepper, sliced

½ red pepper, sliced

1 tbsp browning

1 tbsp tomato ketchup

1 tbsp soy sauce

100ml water

Salt and black pepper, to taste

Chopped coriander, to garnish (optional)

SERVE

Cooked basmati rice (I use golden sella basmati, or grand extra-long)

1. Season the salmon fillets on both sides with the all-purpose seasoning.

2. Heat the oil in a large pan over a medium-high heat, then add the seasoned fish and sear for around 2 minutes on each side. Remove the fish from the pan and set aside on a plate.

3. Add the onion, garlic, Scotch bonnet, thyme and allspice berries to the pan and cook for 2–3 minutes until fragrant. Add the peppers and sauté for another 3 minutes, until they begin to soften.

4. Add the browning, ketchup, soy sauce and water. Stir to combine, then bring the mixture to a simmer. Place the salmon on top of the vegetable mixture. Cover the pan and allow the salmon to steam in the sauce for 3–5 minutes, or until the fish is cooked through and flakes easily.

5. Check the seasoning, adjusting with more salt or pepper if needed.

6. Serve over rice, garnished with some coriander, if you like.

Top Tip I butterfly my salmon for this recipe, as this helps it to cook quicker. To do this, just slice it down the centre horizontally to create two fillets.

SERVES: 6–8 **PREP + COOK TIME: 25 minutes**

SATAY CHICKEN DRUMSTICKS

GF

Let's keep it super simple! These satay drumsticks are about to be your new favourite go-to recipe. As a chef, what I love about this dish is how it hits all the right notes with minimal effort. Juicy drumsticks soak up a rich, nutty marinade, and are then air-fried to crispy goodness in just 25 minutes.

1. Preheat the air fryer to 200°C.
2. In a bowl, whisk together the peanut butter, soy sauce, lime juice, honey, garlic and ginger paste, chilli powder, sesame oil and hot water, and season well with salt and pepper. Stir until smooth and well combined.
3. Add the chicken drumsticks to the satay marinade and turn to generously coat.
4. Arrange the chicken pieces in the air-fryer basket in a single layer and air-fry for 20 minutes, turning halfway to make sure they are evenly cooked.

125g smooth peanut butter

2 tbsp soy sauce (or tamari for gluten-free)

1 tbsp lime juice

1 tbsp honey

1 tbsp garlic and ginger paste

½ tsp chilli powder

1 tsp sesame oil

75ml hot water

12 chicken drumsticks (with or without skin, as preferred)

Salt and black pepper, to taste

Top Tip I love to pair these with the garlicky broccoli or honey glazed carrots.

SERVES: 4–6　　　　　　　　　　　　　　　　　　PREP + COOK TIME: 20 minutes

TURKISH-STYLE PASTA WITH GARLIC YOGHURT

This Turkish-inspired pasta dish went viral. It's a true flavour explosion; it reminds me of all the flavours of the best Turkish kebab in the form of a pasta dish! The combination of savoury meat and tangy garlic yoghurt creates a satisfying meal that hits all the flavours you need in a bowl. I bring everything to the table and let everyone serve themselves more or less of the toppings they like.

1. Cook the pasta in a pan of boiling water, according to the packet instructions. Drain and set aside.
2. While the pasta cooks, prepare the garlic yoghurt by mixing the yoghurt, garlic and a pinch of salt in a bowl. Set aside.
3. For the salsa, toss together the tomatoes, red onion, coriander and lemon juice in a bowl, then season with salt and pepper. Set aside.
4. Heat the oil in a large pan over a medium–high heat. Add the lamb, breaking it up with a spoon until browned and cooked through. This will take around 5 minutes. Add the cumin and paprika, and season with salt and pepper. Stir in the onion and garlic, cooking for another 2–3 minutes until fragrant and softened.
5. Serve the pasta on the table alongside the meat, garlic yoghurt and tomato and coriander salsa, and let everyone layer up their bowls.

400g dried farfalle pasta
2 tbsp olive oil
300g lamb mince
1 tsp ground cumin
1 tsp smoked paprika
½ onion, finely diced
2 garlic cloves, finely minced
Salt and black pepper, to taste

GARLIC YOGHURT

200g thick Greek yoghurt
1 garlic clove, minced

TOMATO AND CORIANDER SALSA

2 large tomatoes, diced
½ red onion, finely chopped
2 sprigs of coriander, chopped
1 tbsp lemon juice

SERVES: 4–6   PREP + COOK TIME: 25 minutes

CHICKEN TRAYBAKE KEBABS

These kebabs are incredibly easy to make, and once you master the marinade, you'll be able to prepare them in no time. The combination of spices and yoghurt makes the chicken incredibly tender and full of flavour, and the traybake method means clean-up is a breeze. You can enjoy these fresh out of the oven or make extra for lunchboxes the next day.

600g chicken mince (see Top Tip)

1 tbsp Greek yoghurt

1 tbsp lemon juice

1 tbsp garlic granules

1 tbsp ground cumin

½ tsp ground turmeric

1 tbsp paprika

1 tbsp vegetable bouillon powder

1 tsp salt

½ tsp ground black pepper

4 sprigs of parsley, finely chopped, plus extra to garnish

Avocado oil spray

4–6 pitta breads (use gluten-free if needed)

Lemon wedges, to serve

ONION AND SUMAC SALAD

2 red onions, sliced into half-moons

Juice of ½ lemon

1 tsp sumac

½ tsp salt

1. Preheat the oven to 200°C fan/220°C/350°F. In a large mixing bowl, combine the chicken mince, yoghurt, lemon juice, garlic granules, spices, bouillon powder, seasoning and parsley, and mix well.

2. Spray a rectangular baking tray with oil. Tip the meat mixture on to the tray and press it down to form a single layer. Cut the meat into 6 rectangles to create the kebabs, then use a knife to score lines in each rectangle to mimic the char marks on a kebab. Bake in the oven for 15 minutes until the kebabs are cooked through and have crispy charred parts on top.

3. While the kebabs are cooking, make the onion salad by combining all the ingredients in a bowl, and warm up the pitta breads.

4. Garnish the meat with fresh parsley and serve hot with the pittas and salad, along with lemon wedges for squeezing.

Top Tip I use chicken thigh mince here, as it has more flavour and I find it helps to stop the kebabs going crumbly.

SERVES: 4 **PREP + COOK TIME: 15 minutes**

FIVE-SPICE BEEF NOODLES

My daughter loves all kinds of noodles, and this recipe is a total hit in our house. It's a super-easy one-pan recipe that comes together in a flash! The combo of fragrant Chinese 5 spice with savoury soy and oyster sauces makes a rich, umami-packed sauce that perfectly coats the noodles. It's the kind of dish that's simple to make but feels really satisfying.

1. Combine all the ingredients for the sauce in a mug. Mix thoroughly and set aside.
2. Heat the oil in a large frying pan over a medium heat. Add the spring onions and garlic and ginger paste, then fry for 1–2 minutes until fragrant and softened.
3. Add the beef mince to the pan, breaking it up with a spatula. Cook for around 5 minutes, until the beef starts to brown, then add the five-spice and cook for a few minutes more until the beef crisps up.
4. Add the cooked noodles to the pan, tossing them with the beef mixture. Pour in the sauce and cook for a few minutes more, until heated through.
5. Serve hot, garnished with extra spring onions, if you like.

1 tbsp vegetable oil

2 spring onions, sliced, plus to serve (optional)

1 tbsp garlic and ginger paste

300g beef mince

1 tbsp Chinese 5 spice

500g cooked egg noodles (or use a ready-made packet)

SAUCE

2 tbsp light soy sauce

1 tbsp dark soy sauce

1 tbsp oyster sauce

1 tsp white caster sugar

100ml vegetable stock

SERVES: 2–4 PREP + COOK TIME: 20 minutes

MISO HONEY AUBERGINE STEAKS

With just a couple of steps, you can have these aubergine steaks ready in about 20 minutes. The air fryer does most of the work for you, making it perfect for when you're short on time but want something flavourful and satisfying. I love to serve these alongside my Honeyed Carrots (see page 160).

1. Cut the aubergines in half lengthways and score a criss-cross pattern on the top of the cut sides, not slicing all the way through. This will allow the flavours to be absorbed into the aubergine flesh. Spray with oil and air-fry for 12 minutes at 200°C.

2. In a small bowl, whisk together the miso paste, honey, soy sauce, rice vinegar, sesame oil, pepper and garlic until smooth and well combined.

3. Once the aubergines are cooked, brush them with this glaze and cook for a further 2 minutes.

4. Serve hot on top of rice or noodles, sprinkled with sesame seeds and spring onions. To finish, drizzle with some crispy chilli oil.

2 aubergines

Avocado oil spray

1 tbsp miso paste

1 tbsp honey

1 tbsp light soy sauce (or tamari for gluten-free)

1 tbsp rice vinegar

1 tbsp sesame oil

½ tsp ground white pepper

4 garlic cloves, minced

SERVE

Black and white sesame seeds

1 spring onion, green part only, chopped

Cooked rice or noodles

Crispy chilli oil

Honeyed carrots (optional) (see page 160)

SERVES: 4 **PREP + COOK TIME: 20 minutes**

CHILLI BEEF BURRITOS WITH 'CHEESE WINGS'

These burritos are a total game-changer, with the 'cheese wings' adding the perfect crunchy umami boost and some excitement to meal times. It gets the kids 'ooohing' and 'aaahhhing' when a big stack of these is brought to the dinner table!

400g beef mince
1 tsp garlic granules
1 tsp smoked paprika
1 tsp ground cumin
½–1 tsp chilli powder (depending on how you like it)
1 tbsp Turkish tomato paste
2 tbsp cornflour
300ml water
Avocado oil spray
Salt and black pepper, to taste

BURRITOS
4 large tortillas
100g Red Leicester cheese, grated
100g mozzarella, grated

SERVE (OPTIONAL)
Soured cream
Salsa
Guacamole

1. Heat a frying pan over a medium heat and add the beef mince, garlic granules, smoked paprika, cumin, chilli powder and tomato paste. Cook for 5 minutes until the mince is crispy.

2. In a small bowl, combine the cornflour and water and mix to create a slurry. Add this to the pan and cook the mixture down until it thickens up; this should take around 3 minutes.

3. Warm the tortillas in the microwave for about 20 seconds.

4. Divide the beef mixture between the tortillas, roll them up tightly, and set aside.

5. Combine the cheeses in a bowl. Wipe the pan with kitchen paper and place it over a medium heat. Sprinkle in a handful of the mixed cheeses to create a circle slightly larger than a burrito. Let it melt and bubble for 30 seconds.

6. Place a burrito seam-side down on to the melted cheese. Let it cook for 1–2 minutes until the cheese turns golden and crispy. Gently lift and flip to crisp on the other side. Repeat to make 'cheese wings' for each burrito.

7. Stack them up and, if you like, serve with soured cream, salsa or guacamole.

EASY
Extras

As much as I love a showstopping main dish, it's the little extras like sides, salads and condiments that I find really elevate a meal. Growing up in a Mauritian family, I was used to having a variety of things on my plate, and for a long time, I convinced myself that a meal wasn't complete unless I had at least 4-5 different dishes served up – which was really stressful to keep up with as life became more complicated with all those extra mouths to feed!

These simple, quick additions (which all take under 30 minutes!) satisfy my Mauritian mama needs to have a few more items on the plate, without all the stress. They're perfect to whip up alongside your main meal or prepare in advance when time's running short. They're also flexible and can be easily customised according to what you've got in your fridge or cupboards, without any extra trips to the shop!

MAKES: 6–8 rotis   PREP + COOK TIME: 25 minutes

VEGGIE ROTIS

Veggie rotis are the perfect way to use up leftover vegetables. I like to make these vibrant broccoli and beetroot rotis as separate; not only are they visually appealing when served together, but they are also each packed with nutrients. The veggies create a soft, flavourful dough that's perfect for dipping, wrapping or serving alongside your favourite curries or stews. Plus, they're quick and easy to make, using ingredients you probably already have on hand.

1. Combine the beetroot or broccoli in a blender with the hot water and blend to form a puree.
2. In a large bowl, combine the flour and salt with your beetroot or broccoli puree. Mix until you have a soft, slightly sticky dough. If it feels too dry, add some hot water, a little at a time; if it's too wet, add a little extra flour. There's no need to knead.
3. Cover the dough with a damp cloth and allow it to rest for 5–10 minutes. This helps to make the dough more pliable.
4. Divide the dough into 6 balls. Lightly dust a work surface with flour, then roll out each ball to form a roti around 20cm in diameter.
5. Heat a frying pan over a medium–high heat. Place one of the rolled-out rotis on to the pan and cook for 1 minute or until bubbles start to form, then flip over and brush or spray the top of the cooked side with oil, then flip it over and cook for another 1–2 minutes, until you see bigger bubbles appear. Brush or spray oil over this side and flip the roti a further two times until it is cooked all the way through.
6. Once cooked, remove the roti from the pan and wrap it in a clean tea towel to steam. This keeps the roti soft and warm until you're ready to serve.
7. Cook the rest of the rotis in the same way. Once cooked, you can also freeze any leftover rotis for later. To reheat, simply defrost one at a time, either in the microwave or in a frying pan.

100g cooked beetroot or cooked broccoli

70ml hot water

300g plain flour, plus extra for dusting

1 tsp salt

50ml vegetable oil, or use a spray for ease

SERVES: 6   PREP + COOK TIME: 15 minutes

QUICK CHEESY NAAN

Everyone I know is obsessed with these cheesy naans, especially when they are fresh out of the pan, as they're soft, fluffy and filled with gooey, melty mozzarella that gives you the most irresistible cheese pull. With no kneading and no resting, the trick to this is using a combination of self-raising flour and yoghurt, to create tender, soft naans.

250g self-raising flour, plus extra for dusting

200g Greek-style full-fat yoghurt

½ tsp salt

150g mozzarella cheese, grated

75g butter

1. In a bowl, combine the self-raising flour, yoghurt and salt, mixing until a dough forms. If it's sticky, add a little more flour.

2. Split the dough into 6 equal pieces. Flatten each piece into a small circle, place a portion of mozzarella in the centre of each, then bring up the edges of the dough to form a parcel around the cheese and seal by pinching the edges together to make 6 balls.

3. On a lightly floured work surface, gently roll out each stuffed dough ball into a naan shape about 5mm thick.

4. Heat a dry frying pan over a medium heat. Cook the naans, one at a time, for 2–3 minutes on each side until golden brown and puffed up.

5. Once each naan comes out of the pan, grab your butter straight from the packet and generously wipe it over both sides of the bread, then cover with a clean tea towel to keep warm while you cook the rest. Make sure to butter each one as soon as it comes out.

6. Serve warm with curry, chutney or on their own.

SERVES: 4   PREP + COOK TIME: 5 minutes

GARLICKY LEMON BROCCOLI

Once I realised how useful my microwave was, I started experimenting with it, and that's when I discovered the ultimate broccoli hack! My daughter has always loved two vegetables the most – cucumbers and broccoli – and I've never had to worry about her not eating them, even when she's not feeling well. This is, by far, the side we have the most often; it's on our table at least four nights a week. The best part? It's ready in less than five minutes! Plus, any leftovers stay fresh in the same container I cooked it in, ready for tomorrow's meal.

350g broccoli florets (I always use Tenderstem or similar here)

1 tsp garlic granules

Zest and juice of ½ lemon

1 tbsp extra virgin olive oil

½ tsp salt, or to taste

1. Place the broccoli florets in a microwave-safe bowl, then sprinkle over the garlic granules.

2. Cover the bowl with a microwave-safe lid and microwave on High for 3½ minutes, until the broccoli is tender and bright green.

3. Once the broccoli is cooked, remove it from the microwave and drain any excess water. Drizzle with the lemon zest and juice, extra virgin olive oil and salt. Toss it all together, then serve on the table in the container you've cooked it in!

SERVES: 4 **PREP + COOK TIME: 5 minutes, plus 1 day marinating**

PIMA CRAZER – MAURITIAN CHILLI SAUCE

The only chilli sauce you'll ever need! Packed with heat and flavour, this sauce is made from chillies, garlic, lemon, vinegar and salt: simple ingredients that really bring all your meals to life. It's a chilli sauce that literally hits you in the face, so don't expect this to be mild. It punches with heat and slaps you with sour. When I make this, I usually double the recipe, because I have to make sure my sister stays stocked up throughout the year! I like to serve it with my Chicken Jollof (see page 72) and Mauritian Noodles (see page 62).

1. Blend all the ingredients in a food processor until the mixture is well combined. You don't want a smooth paste, you still want to see some texture.
2. Adjust the seasoning to taste, adding more lemon or vinegar if you prefer more tang.
3. Transfer to a jar and refrigerate. Let the flavours develop for at least a day before using. Store for up to a month, making sure to top up the oil as you use it.

20 red bird's-eye chillies, chopped

2 garlic cloves, minced

2 tbsp vegetable oil

½ lemon, cut into cubes, skin on, pips removed

1 tbsp white vinegar

½ tsp salt

1 tsp white caster sugar

SERVES: 4 **PREP + COOK TIME: 45 minutes**

THE BEST ROAST POTATOES

The hack of all hacks for the crispiest roast potatoes! By starting them off in the microwave, you cut down on cooking time (and washing-up) while guaranteeing the perfect fluffy interiors. A quick blast in the air fryer gives them the most ridiculously crunchy exteriors. No boiling, no cooling down, no searing the potatoes in hot oil – just foolproof roasties every time!

1. Place the chopped potatoes in a microwave-safe bowl and microwave on High for 8 minutes until they start to soften.

2. Drain any liquid from the potatoes, then spray with oil and sprinkle generously with salt. Add the thyme sprigs, cover the container with a lid and shake the potatoes to evenly coat them in the oil seasoning. This will also break down some of the potatoes, which is perfect for the those extra-crispy bits we all fight over.

3. Transfer to the air fryer and cook at 190°C for 25–30 minutes, shaking halfway through for an even crunch. If you see the potatoes drying out, spray with some more oil and keep cooking.

- 4 potatoes (about 600g total), peeled and cut into thirds
- Avocado oil spray
- Salt, to taste
- A few sprigs of thyme

SERVES: 4   PREP + COOK TIME: 15 minutes

HONEYED CARROTS

The easiest, most delicious way to make perfectly roasted carrots! By par-cooking them in the microwave first, you speed up the process – then you just let the air fryer work its magic for a beautifully caramelised finish. A drizzle of honey, oregano and salt takes them to the next level, making them sweet, savoury and irresistible!

400g carrots, peeled and halved
1 tbsp olive oil
1 tbsp honey
½ tsp dried oregano
½ tsp salt, or to taste

1. Place the carrots in a microwave-safe bowl and microwave on High for 3-4 minutes until slightly softened. Drain any water.
2. Toss the carrots with the olive oil and air-fry at 190°C for 12 minutes, shaking halfway through.
3. Drizzle the carrots with the honey and sprinkle with the oregano and salt, then return to the air fryer for 3 minutes more until caramelised.

SERVES: 2–4

PREP + COOK TIME: 10 minutes

PLANTAINS

Plantains are one of the best naturally sweet snacks you can find! Whether you pan-fry or air-fry them, here's how to get them just right every time. The only issue is that I always assign the rule 'one for the cook, one for the guest' while cooking, so you may want to double up on this recipe if you think you might dip into the stash while you're cooking too!

TO PAN-FRY

1. Cut the plantains into 5mm diagonal slices (this increases surface area) and season with salt.
2. Heat the oil in a frying pan over a medium heat and fry the plantains for 2–3 minutes per side until golden brown and caramelised.
3. Drain on paper towels, sprinkle with salt and enjoy hot.

TO AIR-FRY

1. Cut the plantains into 5mm diagonal slices and season with salt. Spray generously with avocado oil.
2. Air-fry at 190°C for 10 minutes, turning halfway during cooking.

TO PAN-FRY

2 ripe plantains, peeled (see Top Tip)

1 tbsp oil

Salt, to taste

TO AIR-FRY

2 ripe plantains, peeled (see Top Tip)

Avocado oil spray

Salt, to taste

Top Tip When choosing plantains, look for ones with large black spots on the skin, as this indicates that they're ripe and sweet! If the plantain is still green, you'll need to wait 1–2 weeks for it to ripen. To speed up the ripening process, try placing it next to an avocado in your fruit bowl. Once the skin has darkened, the plantain is easier to peel – and if you notice a sweet, fragrant smell when you peel, this means it's ready to be enjoyed!

SERVES: 4 **PREP + COOK TIME: 15 minutes**

SWEETCORN RIBS

This used to be one of the most popular starters at my restaurant, but also the one that my team loathed to make, mainly because it's easy for the corn to break when you're cutting the cobs and we needed each 'rib' to be perfect! When at home, you don't need to stress too much about things being perfect. Be warned, though, this does get messy, and you'll need a toothpick and wet wipes after dinner – but it's worth it.

2 corn on the cob, quartered lengthways
1 tbsp tamarind paste
1 tbsp tomato ketchup
1 tbsp soy sauce (or tamari for gluten-free)
1 tsp maple syrup
1 tsp garlic granules
1 tbsp olive oil

SERVE
Black and white sesame seeds
Chopped spring onions

1. Place the corn in the air fryer and cook at 190°C for 10 minutes.
2. Add the tamarind paste, ketchup, soy sauce, maple syrup, garlic granules and olive oil. Shake everything around until the corn is evenly coated in the glaze, then cook for a further 3 minutes.
3. Remove from the air fryer and serve hot, sprinkled with sesame seeds and spring onions for that extra flavour kick.

SERVES: 4   PREP + COOK TIME: 15 minutes, plus 1 day marinating

ZASAR LEGIM – SPICY MAURITIAN PICKLED VEGETABLES

Zasar Legim is the Mauritian answer to kimchi: a vibrant, tangy and slightly spicy pickle that's packed with probiotics and bursting with flavour. Made with white cabbage, green beans and carrots, it's the kind of thing you'll find in almost every Mauritian fridge in a repurposed butter tub! It keeps beautifully for up to two weeks in the fridge – but trust me, it never lasts that long because it's just too addictive. In fact, as I am writing this, I have realised that my tub is empty, and I need to go and make some more!

1. Put the chopped vegetables in a heatproof bowl and pour over enough freshly boiled water to cover, then leave to sit for 2 minutes just to blanch. Tip into a colander and drain, then rinse under cold water. Dry the vegetables with a tea towel and set aside.

2. Using a pestle and mortar, crush the mustard seeds and garlic together. Heat the oil in a pan for a minute, then turn off the heat and add the crushed mustard seeds and garlic to the pan, along with the turmeric, salt, sugar and vinegar. Stir and allow to cool.

3. Now grab some gloves and pour this spice mixture over the blanched vegetables, using your hands to make sure it all gets well coated. (If you don't have gloves to hand, you can use a sandwich bag, but please don't use your bare hands unless you are happy for the turmeric to stain them yellow for a week.)

4. Transfer to a clean container and refrigerate for at least a day before serving for the best flavour.

5. The next day, check the vegetables for flavour, and see if they need more salt or vinegar.

- 200g white cabbage, thinly sliced
- 100g green beans, trimmed and sliced
- 100g carrots, julienned
- 5–10 green chillies, sliced in half
- 1 tbsp mustard seeds
- 2 garlic cloves
- 4 tbsp vegetable oil
- ½ tsp ground turmeric
- 1 tsp salt, or to taste
- ½ tsp caster sugar
- 2–3 tbsp white vinegar

SERVES: 4   PREP + COOK TIME: 20 minutes

EVERYDAY RICE

This is what I call a Ping and Go recipe: just press start on the microwave and forget about it! In under 20 minutes you'll have perfectly fluffy rice. Growing up, we always had a rice cooker, and while I love having one, I've found that with all the other gadgets at home, it takes up so much space. When I realised I could get the same result using the microwave, it was a no-brainer. I haven't used a rice cooker since! No fuss, no stirring, just delicious results every time. And the best part for me is that whatever you cook the rice in is the same container I use to store the leftovers in the fridge, so there's no extra washing up!

300g basmati rice
420ml water
½ tsp salt

1. Rinse the rice in a sieve under cold running water until the water runs clear (see Top Tip). Transfer to a large microwave-safe bowl and add the water and salt.
2. Cover the bowl with a microwave-safe lid or plate and microwave on High for 15–17 minutes.
3. Remove from the microwave and use a fork to fluff up the rice.
4. Let the rice sit, covered, until you are ready to serve.

Top Tip Rinsing the rice removes starch and stops the grains from sticking together.

SERVES: 4   PREP + COOK TIME: 20 minutes

GOLDEN SPICED RICE

This uses exactly the same method as for the Everyday rice. I love to make this regularly, as I find the pop of yellow rice on the plate make mealtimes so appealing!

300g basmati rice
420ml water
½ tsp salt
1 tsp vegetable bouillon powder
1 tsp cumin seeds
½ tsp ground turmeric
Chopped coriander

1. Rinse the rice in a sieve under cold running water until the water runs clear (see Top Tip).
2. Transfer to a large microwave-safe bowl and add the water, salt, bouillon powder, cumin seeds and turmeric. Cover the bowl with a microwave-safe lid or plate and microwave on High for 15–17 minutes.
3. Remove from the microwave and use a fork to fluff up the rice. Let the rice sit, covered, until you are ready to serve, then garnish with the coriander.

SERVES: 4   PREP + COOK TIME: 20 minutes

RED RICE

Red rice is one of my favourite dishes because it's rich, comforting and full of bold, familiar flavours. The tomato base infused with paprika and garlic always reminds me of the delicious Turkish rice I've eaten on my many travels across the country. You can easily substitute the rice for bulgur wheat here; the method and quantities can stay the same.

1. Rinse the rice in a sieve under cold running water until the water runs clear (see Top Tip).
2. Transfer to a large microwave-safe bowl and add the water, tomato paste, paprika, garlic and ginger paste and vegetable bouillon powder. Cover the bowl with a microwave-safe lid or plate and microwave on High for 15–17 minutes.
3. Remove from the microwave and use a fork to fluff up the rice. Let the rice sit, covered, until you are ready to serve.

300g basmati rice
420ml water
1 tbsp Turkish tomato paste
1 tbsp paprika
1 tbsp garlic and ginger paste
1 tbsp vegetable bouillon powder

SERVES: 4 **PREP + COOK TIME: 25 minutes**

BATATA HARRA

Batata harra is a vibrant and bold Lebanese-inspired potato dish that's as simple as it is flavourful. The crispy, golden potatoes are air-fried until perfectly crunchy, then tossed with a fragrant mix of garlic, fresh chilli, lemon and salt, creating a wonderful balance of heat and tang. I love to serve them alongside kebabs and grilled meats and fish, they work particularly well with the Air-Fryer Kebabs (see page 122).

1. In a large bowl, toss the potato cubes with olive oil and salt, then place them in the air fryer. Air-fry at 190°C for 20 minutes, shaking halfway to make sure they are crispy on all sides.
2. In a small bowl, mix together the garlic, chilli flakes and lemon zest and juice.
3. Once the potatoes are crispy and golden, transfer them to a bowl and toss with the garlic mixture.
4. Garnish with fresh coriander and serve straightaway.

500g potatoes, peeled and cut into 2cm cubes
3 tbsp olive oil
½ tsp salt
2 garlic cloves, minced
1 tsp chilli flakes
Zest and juice of ½ lemon
Handful of coriander, chopped, to garnish

SWEET
Fixes

I know baking can sometimes feel like a whole big job: so many bowls, spoons and ingredients to measure just right! This section is all about getting your sweet fix, quickly and easily, without all the fuss. You'll find shortcuts and tips that make life in the kitchen a little easier here. These recipes have been tried and tested over the years, and loved by family and friends alike. I don't exactly have a big sweet tooth myself, but there are days, especially when the kids are asking for something sweet, that I need to whip up something quick and tasty. This chapter is my little secret for when that craving hits – for when you hear those familiar words: 'Mama, can I have a snack?'

MAKES: 8 cookies　　　　　　　　　　　　　　PREP + COOK TIME: 15 minutes

MISO CHOCOLATE COOKIES

Adding miso to these cookies gives them an incredibly rich umami depth that pairs perfectly with the sweetness of chocolate. These are a one-bowl wonder, so they're quick and easy to make. Plus, you can freeze the dough and bake them whenever you're in the mood for freshly baked cookies in no time!

1. Preheat your oven to 160°C fan/180°C/350°F and line a baking tray with baking paper.
2. In a large bowl, mix the butter and sugars until smooth and light. Add the egg and miso paste, mixing until fully incorporated. Then add the flour, baking powder and a pinch of salt, mixing until the dough comes together. Lastly, fold in the chocolate chips.
3. Divide the cookie dough into 8 balls and place them on the prepared baking tray, leaving some space between each one to allow for spreading. Bake for 10–12 minutes, or until the edges are golden and the centres are still slightly soft. Let the cookies cool on the tray for a few minutes before transferring them to a wire rack to cool completely. Sprinkle with a little sea salt before serving.

100g unsalted butter, softened
100g light brown soft sugar
50g white caster sugar
1 large egg
2 tbsp white miso paste
200g plain flour
1 tsp baking powder
Pinch of sea salt, plus extra to serve
150g dark chocolate chips

Top Tip You can freeze the cookie dough for later use by rolling it into balls and popping them into a reusable freezer bag. When you're ready for fresh cookies, bake them directly from frozen, adding an extra minute or two to the baking time.

SERVES: 6–8　　　　　　　　　　　　　　　PREP + COOK TIME: 45 minutes

CLASSIC MAURITIAN MASPAIN

A comforting cake often enjoyed in the afternoon or for breakfast with a warm cup of vanilla tea. This cake is similar to an American pound cake or classic vanilla sponge, but with a denser, richer texture. This simple one-bowl method uses oil instead of butter, so it's quick and easy to make.

3 large eggs (see Top Tip)
180g golden caster sugar
120ml vegetable oil
1 tsp vanilla extract
180g self-raising flour
1 tbsp custard powder
½ tsp salt
2–3 tbsp whole milk

1. Preheat the oven to 160°C fan/180°C/350°F and line a 900g loaf tin with baking paper or a loaf liner.

2. In a large mixing bowl, mix the eggs, sugar, oil and vanilla extract until combined. Add the flour, custard powder and salt, along with enough milk to make a smooth batter.

3. Pour the batter into the prepared tin and smooth the top. Bake in the oven for 35–40 minutes, or until a skewer inserted into the centre comes out clean.

4. Let the cake cool in the tin for 10 minutes before transferring it to a wire rack to cool completely.

Top Tip Weigh the eggs before you start; this will give you the correct weight to use for the flour and sugar. I've given approximate weights here, but you can adjust these to match the weight of your eggs.

MAKES: 1   PREP + COOK TIME: 10 minutes

COOKIE FOR MAMA

As a single mum, there are days when I finally finish the bedtime routine, get Niyyah settled in her room, then head back downstairs feeling heavy and drained. I let out a massive sigh, because, let's face it, those days are long and tiring, and I've forgotten to pour back into my own cup! On those nights, I know I need to carve out a little 'me time'. And for me, that often means treating myself. Sometimes all you need is a warm, gooey cookie to wrap up the day on a sweet note. This solo cookie is the perfect quick fix, just for you, when you need a little treat to make the evening feel a little brighter. Making it in your PJs is a compulsory step of the recipe, by the way!

1. In a bowl, combine the butter, both sugars, vanilla extract or powder and salt, and mix until smooth. Add the egg yolk and mix well. Stir in the flour and a pinch of salt, then fold in the chocolate chips.

2. Roll the cookie dough on a small baking sheet, flattening it slightly with your fingers, so that it fits your air-fryer basket, then sprinkle some extra choc chips on top.

3. Air-fry at 180°C for 4–6 minutes, or until the edges are golden but the centre is still soft and gooey. Allow to cool slightly before enjoying warm.

- 1 tbsp soft, room-temperature butter
- 1 tbsp light soft brown sugar
- 1 tbsp white caster sugar
- Drop of vanilla extract or a pinch of vanilla powder
- Pinch of salt
- 1 egg yolk (see Top Tip)
- 3 tbsp plain flour
- 1 tbsp chocolate chips, plus more if you're feeling extra!

Top Tip When separating the egg, save the white for bulking up your omelettes.

MAKES: 4 pockets   PREP + COOK TIME: 20 minutes

AIR-FRYER CHERRY PIE POCKETS

v

Using frozen cherries is the key here. No one has the time to stone cherries, and tinned ones just don't cut it for this recipe; they stay too wet ... and lack that vibrant, fresh cherry flavour that makes this dessert pop. The air fryer speeds up the process, giving you a perfect pie fix in no time.

1. Add the cherries, cornflour, sugar and lemon zest and juice to a saucepan. Cook over a medium heat, stirring constantly, until the cherries defrost and the mixture thickens to become sticky and glossy; this should take a few minutes. Remove from the heat and let it cool – if you are in a rush, spread the mixture out over a large plate and it should cool down in 5 minutes.

2. Roll out the puff pastry sheet on a lightly floured surface and cut it into 4 equal rectangles.

3. Spoon a generous amount of the cooled cherry filling into the centre of one half of each pastry piece. Fold the other half of the pastry over the top, covering the cherry mixture. Use a fork to seal the edges.

4. In a small bowl, beat together the egg yolk and water, then brush this egg wash over each pocket. Slash 3 diagonal slits across the top of each one. Place the pie pockets in the air fryer and cook for 10–12 minutes at 180°C, or until golden brown and crispy.

5. Once the cherry-pie pockets are ready, remove them from the air fryer and serve with a generous drizzle of warm custard or a scoop of ice cream.

200g frozen cherries

1 tbsp cornflour

3 tbsp white caster sugar

Zest and juice of ½ lemon

1 sheet ready-made puff pastry

Plain flour, for dusting

1 egg yolk

1 tsp water

Custard or ice cream, to serve

SERVES: 6–8   PREP + COOK TIME: 45 minutes

PISTACHIO AND ROSE LOAF

This is the recipe everyone requests when I offer to bring something along to a dinner party or event. A beautifully fragrant loaf with the rich flavour of pistachios and the delicate touch of rose, it's a crowd-pleaser every time. The best part? It's a one-bowl bake! Using oil instead of butter and self-raising flour makes it quick and simple to put together.

1. Preheat your oven to 160°C fan/180°C/350°F and line a 900g loaf tin with baking paper or a loaf liner.
2. Put a tablespoon of flour into a small bowl, then stir in the chopped pistachios and set aside.
3. In a large bowl, whisk together the sugar, eggs and oil until smooth and combined. Add the remaining flour, along with the milk, rose water and salt. Mix until just combined, then stir in the floured pistachios (flouring the pistachios stops them from sinking to the bottom of the cake when cooked).
4. Pour the batter into the prepared loaf tin and smooth the top. Bake for 35–40 minutes, or until a skewer inserted in the centre of the loaf comes out clean. Leave to cool in the tin for 10 minutes, then transfer to a wire rack to cool completely.
5. While the cake cools, make the icing by combining the icing sugar and milk or water in a bowl with enough food colouring to get the colour you like.
6. Drizzle the icing over the cooled loaf, then decorate with chopped pistachios and dried rose petals.

200g self-raising flour

100g pistachios, shelled and roughly chopped

160g golden caster sugar

3 large eggs

120ml vegetable oil

100ml whole milk

1 tbsp rose water

Pinch of salt

ICING

150g icing sugar

1–2 tbsp whole milk or water

Small drop of pink food colouring

DECORATE

Dried rose petals

Chopped pistachios

SERVES: 6   PREP + COOK TIME: 25 minutes

WHITE CHOCOLATE AND RASPBERRY TIRAMISU

Ellie Simmonds won *Cooking with the Stars* with this incredible tiramisu, and Michael Caines called it the best tiramisu he'd ever had! Little did he know, this masterpiece was laced with clever shortcuts, but it still tasted like it came straight from a Michelin-starred kitchen. It's the perfect balance of rich, creamy goodness with a hint of coffee and cocoa – plus, it's so much easier than you'd think!

130g white chocolate, roughly chopped
200ml double cream
250g mascarpone
½ tsp vanilla extract or vanilla powder
2 tbsp instant espresso powder
200ml just-boiled water
16–20 sponge fingers, as needed
150g raspberries
Cocoa powder, for dusting

1. Break the white chocolate into pieces and place in a microwave-safe bowl. Microwave on High, in short bursts of 20 seconds, stirring between each one to check whether the chocolate has melted. Once melted, allow to cool and set aside.

2. Combine the double cream and mascarpone in a mixing bowl and whisk by hand until you get soft peaks. Fold in the cooled, melted white chocolate and the vanilla until combined.

3. Dissolve the espresso powder in a shallow dish with the just-boiled water. Dip the sponge fingers into the coffee, letting them soak for a few seconds. Take out 6 glasses or dessert dishes and arrange a layer of coffee-soaked sponge in the base of each. Top with a layer of cream, then another layer of sponge, then finish with another layer of cream. Transfer to the fridge to set for 20 minutes.

4. Finish by decorating with raspberries and dusting the tops with cocoa powder before serving.

MAKES: 12–16 lollies **PREP + COOK TIME: 15 minutes**

MANGO LIME LOLLIES

Every summer, without fail, these lollies are packed into my freezer – a refreshing, tangy treat to beat the heat! Made with sweet tinned Alfonso mango and fresh lime juice, they really are so easy to prepare!

400g tin of Alfonso mango puree

Juice of 2 limes

Handful of raspberries to layer in

1. In a bowl, combine the mango puree and lime juice, and stir well to combine. Pour the mixture into lolly moulds, popping some raspberries in as you go, and leaving a little space at the top for expansion during freezing.

2. Place the moulds into the freezer and freeze for at least 4–6 hours or overnight until solid.

3. To release the lollies, run warm water over the outsides of the moulds for a few seconds, then gently pull the lollies out.

MAKES: 16–20 cookies　　　　　　　　　　　　　　　**PREP + COOK TIME: 15 minutes**

GHRIBA – MOROCCAN COOKIES

I have such fond memories of making these with Niyyah when she was just a baby, and we often bake them during the month of Ramadan or make large batches for Eid and special occasions. I can still picture me running after her trying to wipe down her sticky little icing-sugar-covered hands! These Moroccan cookies are as simple to make as they are delicious, with the delicate fragrance of orange blossom water running throughout. They're the perfect balance of sweet and floral, and the texture is wonderfully crumbly.

1. Preheat your oven to 160°C fan/180°C/350°F and line a baking tray with baking paper.
2. In a large bowl, mix the ground almonds with half the icing sugar, along with the butter, jam, egg and baking powder. Stir until a thick, sticky dough forms.
3. Tip the remaining icing sugar into another large bowl, and pour the orange blossom water into a third bowl.
4. Roll the dough into small balls, each about the size of a walnut, then gently dip each ball first into the orange blossom water, making sure to submerge it, and then into the icing sugar to cover completely.
5. Place the cookies on the baking tray, leaving enough room for them to spread out, and press them down slightly with your fingers. Bake for 12 minutes, or until golden around the edges.
6. Let the cookies cool on the tray for a few minutes before transferring them to a wire rack to cool completely. Store the cookies in an airtight container for up to two weeks.

- 300g ground almonds
- 100g icing sugar
- 50g butter
- 50g apricot jam
- 1 large egg
- 2 tsp baking powder
- 75ml orange blossom water

MAKES: 20–24 diamonds   PREP + COOK TIME: 40 minutes

COCONUT BASBOUSA

This is a deliciously moist and fragrant cake that's beloved across the Middle East and beyond. I was lucky enough to learn this recipe from a wonderful Egyptian friend. There are many variations of this treat; in Morocco, it's drizzled with sweet orange blossom syrup, while in Greece it's known as *revani* and in other regions it's called *namoura* or *hareesa*. Whatever the name, I always order it when I see it on a menu, in any guise! What makes this cake so amazing is how simple it is to prepare; it's a truly forgiving sweet, because even if you mess up the quantities, once it's rested and soaked up the syrup, the flavour is still truly sublime.

3 medium eggs
150g white caster sugar
1 tsp vanilla extract
50g desiccated coconut
100g Greek-style yoghurt
100g soft, room temperature butter
250g coarse semolina
75g plain flour
1 tsp baking powder
Whole almonds, to decorate

SYRUP
150g white caster sugar
150ml water
1 tbsp lemon juice
1 tsp rose water

1. Preheat your oven to 160°C fan/180°C/350°F and line a 20 x 30cm baking tray with baking paper.

2. In a large bowl, combine all the cake ingredients, except the almonds, and mix until you have a thick batter. Pour the batter into the prepared baking tray, spreading it out evenly. Score the top of the batter into diamonds (this helps when cutting after baking) and place one almond in the centre of each diamond. Bake for 30 minutes, or until the cake is golden brown.

3. While the cake is baking, make the syrup by adding the sugar, water and lemon juice to a small saucepan. Bring to the boil, then reduce the heat and simmer for about 10 minutes until slightly thickened. Remove from the heat, then stir in the rose water.

4. Once the cake is out of the oven, immediately pour the syrup evenly over the top, making sure it soaks in.

5. Let the cake cool in the tin, allowing the syrup to fully absorb, before removing it from the tin and cutting it into diamonds. Serve immediately, or store in an airtight container for up to two weeks.

MAKES: 8 doughnuts **PREP + COOK TIME: 15 minutes**

CINNAMON DOUGHNUTS

These vegan cinnamon doughnuts are a total game-changer – light, fluffy and coated in a sweet cinnamon sugar that will melt in your mouth. Plus, they're made in the air fryer, so there's no need for deep-frying or a mess. Quick, easy and perfectly spiced!

1. In a bowl, stir together the self-raising flour and yoghurt until you have a sticky dough. Depending on the brand or thickness of the yoghurt, you may need to add slightly more or less flour to reach the correct consistency. Flour your hands and split the dough into 8 pieces, rolling each one into a ball. Using your thumb and index finger, groove out a hole in the middle of each one to create doughnuts.

2. Lightly spray the air fryer basket as well as the doughnuts themselves with a little oil. Place 4 doughnuts in the basket in a single layer, leaving space between them because they will puff out and expand when cooking. Air-fry at 180°C for 8–10 minutes, then repeat with the second batch.

3. While the doughnuts are cooling slightly, mix together the caster sugar and cinnamon in a shallow dish.

4. Once the doughnuts are warm but not too hot, dip them into the cinnamon sugar mixture, making sure they are coated evenly. Serve immediately, or store in an airtight container for up to two days.

300g self-raising flour
250g coconut yoghurt
Avocado oil spray

CINNAMON SUGAR
50g golden caster sugar
½ tsp ground cinnamon

SERVES: 12 **PREP + COOK TIME: 30 minutes**

CRINKLE BAKLAVA TRAY

I absolutely love baklava, but the effort it takes to make it the traditional way is reserved for my long and lazy weekends (whenever that happens – insert eye-roll here!). So, this Crinkle Baklava Tray is a super-easy version of the traditional dessert that you can make even on the busiest of midweek nights.

1. Preheat your oven to 160°C fan/180°C/350°F and grease a 20 x 30cm baking tray.
2. Lay one sheet of filo pastry across the tray, then scrunch it up lengthways, concertina-style. Pour a little melted butter over the filo. Repeat this process, continuing to crinkle and stack each new filo sheet on top of the last, buttering each layer as you go. Don't worry about making it neat – the crinkles will give it that rustic look!
3. Once all the filo is in the tray, sprinkle the crushed walnuts evenly over the top. Bake for 20–25 minutes, or until golden and crispy.
4. While the baklava is baking, prepare the sugar syrup. Combine the caster sugar, water and lemon juice in a saucepan. Bring to a simmer over a medium heat and cook for about 10 minutes until slightly thickened.
5. Once the baklava is golden and crispy, remove it from the oven. While it's still hot, pour the sugar syrup evenly over the top, making sure it soaks into the layers.
6. Let the baklava cool completely in the tin, then cut it into rectangles and serve.

10 sheets of filo pastry
150g butter, melted
80g walnuts, crushed

SUGAR SYRUP
150g white caster sugar
150ml water
1 tbsp lemon juice

MAKES: 12–16 slices PREP + COOK TIME: 30 minutes

FUNFETTI TRAYBAKE

This is a true crowd-pleaser! It's a one-bowl wonder, meaning less mess and more fun. It's baked in just 25 minutes and always turns out perfectly, thanks to a simple trick – just weigh the eggs, and use the same weight for all the other ingredients. So easy and foolproof. Plus, it's cooked in a disposable foil tray, making it perfect for taking to parties or picnics without the worry of losing your container!

3 large eggs (see Top Tip)
Soft, room-temperature butter
White caster sugar
Self-raising flour
1 tsp vanilla extract
¼ tsp salt
1–2 tbsp whole milk (optional, to loosen the batter)
30g funfetti sprinkles, plus extra to decorate

ICING
150g icing sugar
1–2 tbsp whole milk

1. Preheat your oven to 160°C fan/180°C/350°F. Line a 20 x 30cm disposable foil tray with baking paper or lightly grease it.

2. Weigh your eggs, then measure out equal quantities of butter, caster sugar and flour based on the egg weight for perfect balance.

3. Add the eggs, butter, sugar, flour, vanilla and salt to a mixing bowl and stir until just combined. If the batter is too thick, add a splash of milk to loosen it up.

4. Gently fold in the sprinkles, ensuring they're evenly distributed throughout the batter.

5. Pour the batter into the prepared tray and smooth it out evenly. Bake in the oven for 20–25 minutes, or until a toothpick inserted into the centre comes out clean and the top is golden.

6. Leave the cake too cool completely in the tray. Meanwhile, make the icing by combining the icing sugar with enough milk to get your preferred consistency. Once the cake is cool, drizzle the icing generously over the top, then scatter with sprinkles to finish. You can store the cake in an airtight container for up to 5 days.

Top Tip Weigh the eggs before you start, and this will give you the correct weight to use for the butter, sugar and flour.

SERVES: 8 PREP + COOK TIME: 15 minutes

AIR-FRYER S'MORES

These s'mores are perfect for when you have a group of kids over! They're easy, fun and interactive, as everyone can dunk their biscuits into a gooey, melty chocolate and marshmallow tray. Great for a quick treat that will keep everyone entertained!

1. Arrange the chocolate in the base of a cake tin that will fit inside your air fryer, then top with the marshmallows.

2. Place the tin in the air fryer and cook for 5–7 minutes at 180°C, or until the marshmallows are golden brown and have expanded and the chocolate has melted. Remove from the air fryer and let cool slightly.

3. Place the tray on the table and let everyone dip into the S'mores, just like you would with nachos, using the digestive biscuits to scoop up the gooey goodness.

300g dark chocolate, broken into pieces

200 giant marshmallows (I use Dandies, because they are vegan)

8 digestive biscuits, to serve

SERVES: 10–12   PREP + COOK TIME: 15 minutes

SWISS ROLL CAKE

I didn't want to gatekeep this major cheat; in fact I literally sent a WhatsApp video to all my friends when I came up with this hack! I was so delighted, I couldn't stop laughing. Let's be honest, it's not really a recipe – it's more of a genius shortcut! This simple dessert looks stunning, and is perfect for last-minute parties or get-togethers in your busy midweek. All you need is a shop-bought Swiss roll, cream and berries. You'll be laughing to yourself too when it's on the table!

3 shop-bought Swiss rolls (chocolate or plain jam) or 2 jumbo Swiss Rolls

600ml double cream

Fresh berries, for decoration (see Top Tip)

1. Slice the Swiss roll into pieces about 8–12cm thick, depending on the length of your Swiss roll. The larger your pieces, the taller your cake, so it depends on what type of impact you want to make!

2. Arrange the slices in a circular pattern on a serving plate, making sure to leave a little space between each piece. Once you've arranged the Swiss roll slices, pour your double cream into a metal bowl and whisk until you can see soft peaks. Now you have whipped cream. Cover your Swiss roll slices generously with the cream, making sure to fill in the gaps and smooth it over the top.

3. Decorate with fresh berries and pop into the fridge until you are ready to serve.

4. When you cut into the cake, you'll see those beautiful horizontal lines from the Swiss rolls, creating a stunning effect that will wow your guests.

Top Tip If you prefer, you can use funfetti sprinkles to decorate, or whatever you have at home.

MAKES: 18–20 pieces   PREP + COOK TIME: 15 minutes

EASY PISTACHIO BARFI

The first time I made this recipe, I shocked myself at how quick it was! It's so simple. These are super addictive, so make sure to pack them away quickly, or you might end up eating them all yourself!

1. Line a 15 x 20cm glass tray with baking paper. Gently heat the condensed milk in a non-stick saucepan over a medium heat for 2–3 minutes, stirring occasionally to prevent burning.
2. Stir in the milk powder, ground pistachios, cardamom and salt, and cook for another 2–4 minutes, allowing the mixture to thicken and come away at the sides like a thick dough.
3. Tip out the dough into the prepared tray and press it down firmly to flatten. Tumble over the chopped pistachios, and finish with some gold leaf for extra razzle-dazzle!
4. Leave to cool in the freezer for 1 hour or in the fridge for 2–3 hours, then cut it into small squares or diamonds. Store out on the counter for up to 7 days.

397g tin of sweetened condensed milk

150g milk powder

100g pistachios, shelled and blended to a fine powder

½ tsp ground cardamom

Pinch of salt

DECORATE

Shelled and chopped pistachios

Gold leaf

MAKES: 8 pieces   PREP + COOK TIME: 15 minutes

MICROWAVE SHORTBREAD

This is the easiest shortbread recipe ever! You mix everything in the same container that you microwave it in, and in just 4 minutes you'll have delicious, melt-in-your-mouth shortbread. No fuss, no mess – just the perfect treat in no time! I make this in my 15 x 20cm glass roaster, which is perfect for the microwave, and has a clip-and-seal lid to keep the shortbread fresh after cooking!

1. Tip the butter into a 15 x 20cm microwave-safe dish, and microwave on High in 10-second bursts, stirring between each one until the butter has melted. Then add the flour, sugar and salt, and mix everything together until you have a dough-like consistency.

2. Flatten the dough in the container in an even layer. You can use a spoon or your fingers to press it down evenly, Use a fork to prick the top of the dough in several places, then use a knife to cut the dough into 8 rectangles.

3. Microwave on High for 3–4 minutes. Keep an eye on it, as microwaves vary in power. When it's ready, the shortbread should be firm to the touch. Bear in mind that the colour won't change much.

4. Let the shortbread cool in the container for a few minutes before sprinkling over some caster sugar and serving warm. Otherwise, you can allow to cool completely, then store for up to 3 days in an airtight container at room temperature.

200g plain flour

50g white caster sugar, plus extra to finish

Pinch of salt

100g butter, melted

SERVES: 12   PREP + COOK TIME: 15 minutes

THE ULTIMATE CHOCOLATE CAKE IN 15 MINUTES!

This microwave chocolate cake recipe is the ultimate time-saving hack! You can stir the batter and cook it all in the same glass dish, then take it straight to the table to serve! Cooking this cake in the microwave makes it soft and tender, almost like a steamed dessert, with a rich flavour that makes each bite indulgent. This cake is so decadent that a little goes a long way, so it's perfect for satisfying your sweet tooth without overdoing it.

150ml whole milk
1 medium egg
100g golden caster sugar
1 tsp vanilla extract
125g self-raising flour
2 tbsp cocoa powder
½ tsp salt

ICING

150g icing sugar
2 tbsp cocoa powder
2 tbsp whole milk
Pinch of salt

1. In a 26cm microwave-safe baking dish, whisk together the milk, egg, sugar, vanilla, flour, cocoa powder and salt until smooth and combined.

2. Wipe down the edges of the dish to clean it up, then microwave the batter on High for 8–10 minutes, until fully cooked. Allow the cake to rest while you prepare the icing.

3. In a bowl, whisk together the icing ingredients until smooth. Pour the icing over the top of the cake and allow it to set.

4. Once the icing has set, cut the cake into slices and serve! You can store this in an airtight container for up to 5 days.

Cook Your Way: APPLIANCE GUIDE

To help you find what you need even faster here's a handy list of recipes grouped by appliance or dietary requirement so you can plan around what you have in your kitchen and how you like to eat.

AIR FRYER RECIPES

16	Loaded Breakfast Quiche
27	Golden Air-fryer Muffins
37	Chipotle Chicken Bowl
40	Mango and Halloumi Shake-up Salad
42	Crispy Rice Salad
46	Harissa Roasted Pumpkin and Chickpeas
100	Air-fried Chicken
122	Air-fryer Kebabs
139	Satay Chicken Drumsticks
146	Miso Honey Aubergine Steaks
158	The Best Roast Potatoes
160	Honeyed Carrots
161	Plantains
162	Sweetcorn Ribs
168	Batata Harra
174	Cookie for Mama
176	Air-fryer Cherry Pie Pockets
186	Cinnamon Doughnuts
192	Air-fryer S'mores

GLUTEN-FREE RECIPES

18	Coconut Mango Overnight Oats
20	Speedy Masala Beans
21	Creamy Corn Pudding
30	Chilla – Chickpea and Spinach Pancakes
36	Chipotle Chicken Bowl
39	Sticky Mushroom Rice
42	Crispy Rice Salad
46	Harissa Roasted Pumpkin and Chickpeas
54	Green Biriyani
64	Black Bean Stew with Plantain
76	Prawns in Creole Sauce
100	Air-fried Chicken
121	Domoda – Peanut Stew with Okra and Sweet Potato
186	Cinnamon Doughnuts

MICROWAVE RECIPES

20	Speedy Masala Beans
26	Spicy Egg Bagel
45	Creamy Coconut Tomato Daal
132	Cheesy Microwave Mac Magic
198	Microwave Shortbread

VEGAN/VEGETARIAN RECIPES

18	Coconut Mango Overnight Oats (Ve)
20	Speedy Masala Beans (V)
28	Fluffy Yoghurt Pancakes (V)
30	Chilla – Chickpea and Spinach Pancakes (Ve)
38	Fresh and Crunchy Summer Rolls (Ve)
42	Creamy Coconut Tomato Daal (Ve)
45	Crispy Rice Salad (Ve)
46	Harissa Roasted Pumpkin and Chickpeas (Ve)
178	Pistachio & Rose Loaf (V)
183	Ghriba – Moroccan Cookies (V)
190	Funfetti Traybake (V)

INGREDIENT SHARING: DON'T WASTE IT!

This section shows you which recipes share the same ingredients so you can shop smarter, reduce waste, and stretch ingredients across meals.

HALF A BLOCK OF CHEESE
- 16 Loaded Breakfast Quiche
- 81 Paratha Chilli Cheese Rolls
- 154 Quick Cheesy Naan
- 198 Cheesy Microwave Mac Magic

OPENED CAN OF COCONUT MILK
- 18 Coconut Mango Overnight Oats
- 45 Creamy Coconut Tomato Daal
- 68 Cajun Seafood Stew

SPINACH OR FROZEN GREENS
- 30 Chilla - Chickpea and Spinach Pancakes
- 42 Crispy Rice Salad
- 54 Green Biriyani

JAR OF HARISSA OR RED CURRY PASTE
- 26 Spicy Egg Bagel
- 46 Harissa Roasted Pumpkin and Chickpeas
- 66 Lamb Meatball Red Thai Curry

GARLIC/GINGER PASTE
- 46 Harissa Roasted Pumpkin and Chickpeas
- 58 Creamy Garlic Chicken Pasta
- 70 Mauritian Roti Beef
- 80 Tuna Suugo with Baasta

SHELINA'S 7 DAY MEAL PLAN

	BREAKFAST	LUNCH	DINNER	SWEET FIX
MON	Spicy Egg Bagel page 26	Chipotle Chicken Bowl page 36	Chicken Jollof page 72	Air-fryer Cherry Pie Pockets page 176
TUES	Coconut Mango Overnight Oats page 18	Creamy Coconut Tomato Daal page 45	Creamy Garlic Chicken Pasta page 58	Coconut Basbousa page 184
WED	Chilla – Chickpea and Spinach Pancakes page 30	Harissa Roasted Pumpkin and Chickpeas page 46	Lamb Meatball Red Thai Curry page 66	Crinkle Baklava Tray page 188
THURS	Golden Air-fryer Muffins page 27	Sticky Mushroom Rice page 39	Mauritian Roti Beef page 70	Ghriba – Moroccan Cookies page 183
FRI	Pistachio Croissants page 24	Fresh and Crunchy Summer Rolls page 38	Chicken Peri Peri Traybake page 106	Funfetti Traybake page 190
SAT	Creamy Corn Pudding page 21	Pineapple Fried Rice with Cashews page 78	Black Bean Stew with Plantain page 64	Air-fryer S'mores page 192
SUN	Loaded Breakfast Quiche page 16	Crispy Rice Salad page 42	Cajun Seafood Stew page 68	The Ultimate Chocolate Cake in 15 Minutes! page 200

NOW, FILL IN YOUR OWN!

	BREAKFAST	LUNCH	DINNER	SWEET FIX
MON				
TUES				
WED				
THURS				
FRI				
SAT				
SUN				

GET TO KNOW YOUR SPICES

Spices don't just bring heat, they build flavour. Becoming confident in using them is just a matter of time and using them regularly while cooking. A pinch of cumin can warm a soup, and a hint of cinnamon can transform a curry. Here's a simple cheat sheet:

SPICE	FLAVOUR	TRY MY…	Page
GROUND CUMIN	Earthy, warm	Harissa Roasted Pumpkin and Chickpeas Green Biriyani	46 54
GROUND CORIANDER	Fresh, citrusy	Moroccan Vegetable Tagine Air-fryer Kebabs	104 122
GROUND TURMERIC	Bitter, musky	Creamy Coconut Tomato Daal Mauritian Moulouktani Chicken	45 120
GARAM MASALA	Sweet, aromatic blend	Speedy Masala Beans Prawn Butter Masala	20 108
CURRY POWDER	Bold, complex	Roti Canai Eggs With a Mango Twist Five-Ingredient Coconut Chicken Curry	22 124
PAPRIKA	Sweet or smoky	Creamy Garlic Chicken Pasta Chicken Jollof	58 72
ALLSPICE/ CINNAMON	Sweet-spicy depth	Coconut Mango Overnight Oats Prawn and Plantain Curry Saturday Soup with Dumplings	18 102 110

Top Tip I always like to add whole spices at the beginning of recipes and toast them before adding other ingredients. Ground spices are usually more versatile, but still need heat to reactivate them and bring out their essential oils, which is where all the flavours live.

HOW TO STORE SPICES LIKE A PRO

Keep them in airtight jars
away from direct light, heat or steam.

Use a spice drawer, shelf or turntable
whatever keeps them easy to reach while cooking.

Don't store them above the hob or kettle!
This is a common mistake, but moisture kills flavour, so these steamy areas are not suitable for spices.

Buy your spices in small amounts unless you use a lot.
Label jars and give them a sniff before use; if they've lost their fragrance, it's usually a good indication that they have lost their life and need to be binned!

Keep your everyday staples close to hand.

Store any bulk spice bags in the freezer to preserve flavour.
This works particularly well for those spices you use less of, and also works for whole spices. I do the same with chillies, ginger and garlic; it's a great way to reduce food waste and preserve the flavours.

BATCH-COOKING TIPS

Whether you're cooking for one, feeding a small family, or just don't want to cook every day, mastering leftovers and batch cooking is a total game-changer. Save time, money and stress while still eating deliciously. These tips are everything I have learned during more than a decade spent running my own professional kitchen. I hope they will help you get on top of batch cooking!

TOP BATCH-COOKING RECIPES FROM THIS BOOK

These dishes freeze well and reheat easily, making them perfect for batch cooking.

Page	TRY MY...	GREAT FOR...
39	Sticky Mushroom Rice	Making rice balls for kids
45	Creamy Coconut Tomato Daal	Thermos lunches
46	Harissa Roasted Pumpkin and Chickpeas	Enjoying hot or cold
54	Green Biriyani	A vegan feast
58	Creamy Garlic Chicken Pasta	An easy all-in-one meal
64	Black Bean Stew with Plantain	Comfort food, filling the fridge
72	Chicken Jollof	Feeding (and pleasing) a crowd

COOKING FOR SMALLER FAMILIES OR SOLO?

Don't simply halve the quantities to try and make half the recipe; this doesn't always work, especially when you are cooking with spices and other flavours. My advice is to make the full recipe, then divide it into portions and freeze some for another day.

Batch cooking isn't about being perfect or seeing how everyone else does it on social media. It's about giving your future-self a hug, so you get some peace in the day. Some days you'll cook, and on the other days you'll just reheat and rest. That's exactly what I want for you.

SIMPLE FREEZER STORAGE RULES

Cool foods quickly.

Get your food into the freezer within 1 hour after cooking.

Use clear containers and label everything.

This way you know exactly what you have, and it's easy to see everything when you open the freezer.

Date your freezer meals.

Mark the labels with the date as well as the contents, and rotate the containers in your freezer so older items are brought to the front.

Reheat properly.

Reheated foods should be piping hot.

Freeze sauces, stews and rice dishes in portions.

Freezing them once already portioned makes it easy to defrost and reheat the right quantity.

Keep pancakes, muffins and wraps between layers of baking paper.

Then stack in bags or tubs so they don't stick together. This makes it easy to take one out at a time as needed. This also works for cookies and roti.

Always have a stash of microwave-safe glass containers.

This makes reheating meals a breeze.

Don't refreeze anything that's already been frozen and reheated.

Index

air fryer recipes 204
    air-fried chicken 100, **101**
    air-fryer cherry pie pockets **176**, 177
    air-fryer kebabs 122, **123**
    air-fryer s'mores **192**, 193
    the best roast potatoes **158**, 159
    crispy rice salad 42
    golden air-fryer muffins 27
    harissa roasted pumpkin and chickpeas 46, **47**
    mango and halloumi shake-up salad **40**, 41
    sweetcorn ribs 162, **163**
    all in one pot 52–73
almond (ground), ghriba – Moroccan cookies 183
appliance guide 204
aubergine
    miso honey aubergine steaks **146**, 147
    Turkish lamb and aubergine traybake 71
avocado 37

baasta, tuna suugo with 80
bagel, spicy egg 26
baklava, crinkle baklava tray **188**, 189
barfi, easy pistachio **196**, 197, **202**
basbousa, coconut 184, **185**
batata harra **168**, 169
batch cooking 10, 210
bean(s) 37, 42, 165
    black bean stew with plantain 64
    speedy masala beans 20
beef
    air-fryer kebabs 122, **123**
    Cevapi – juicy grilled Balkan kebabs **84**, 85
    chilli beef with broccoli 90, **91**
    chilli beef burritos with 'cheese wings' 148, **149**
    corned beef rougaille 88
    five-spice beef noodles **144**, 145
    Mauritian roti beef 70
    spaghetti Bolognese **128**, 129
berries 27, 194
    see also raspberry
besan flour 31
biriyani, green **54**, 55

biscuits
    shortbread **198**, 199
    see also cookies
black bean 37
    black bean stew with plantain 64
Bolognese **128**, 129
bread
    pull-apart pizza rolls **98**, 99
    Turkish pizza bread 83
breakfasts 14–31
broccoli 55, 56, 153
    chilli beef with broccoli 90, **91**
    garlicky lemon broccoli 156
bulgar pilaf, chicken 65
burritos, chilli beef burritos with 'cheese wings' 148, **149**

cabbage 42, 86, 105, 165
    savoury cabbage pancakes **94**, 95
Cajun seafood stew 68, **69**
cakes
    funfetti traybake 190, **191**, **202–3**
    pistachio and rose loaf **178**, 179
    Swiss roll cake 194, **195**, **202**
    the ultimate chocolate cake in 15 minutes! 200, **201**
cardamom 21, 197
carrot 38, 62, 86, 110, 121
    honeyed carrots 160
    Mauritian carrot and red lentil soup 115
    Moroccan vegetable tagine **104**, 105
    zasar legim **164**, 165
cashew nut with pineapple fried rice 78, **79**
cassava 55, 110
Cevapi – juicy grilled Balkan kebabs **84**, 85
Cheddar cheese
    cheesy microwave mac magic 132, **133**
    loaded breakfast quiche **16**, 17, **32–3**
cheese
    cheesy microwave mac magic 132, **133**
    chilli beef burritos with 'cheese wings' 148, **149**
    creamy garlic chicken pasta **58**, 59
    mango and halloumi shake-up salad **40**, 41

paratha chilli-cheese rolls **82**, 91
quick cheesy naan 154, **155**
see also Cheddar cheese; mascarpone; mozzarella cheese
cherry pie pockets, air-fryer **176**, 177
chicken
    air-fried chicken 100, **101**
    chicken bulgur pilaf 65
    chicken jollof **72**, 73
    chicken peri peri traybake 106, **107**
    chicken shawarma **134**, 135
    chicken traybake kebabs 142, **143**
    chipotle chicken bowl **36**, 37
    creamy garlic chicken pasta **58**, 59
    five-ingredient coconut chicken curry **124**, 125
    Mauritian moon fan braised chicken rice **60**, 61
    Mauritian Moulouktani chicken 120
    nasi goreng **130**, 131
    satay chicken drumsticks 139
    Thai coconut curry noodle soup 136, **137**
chickpea(s)
    chilla – chickpea and spinach pancakes **30**, 31
    domoda – peanut stew with okra and sweet potato 121
    harissa roasted pumpkin and chickpeas **46**, 47
    Moroccan harira 114
    Moroccan vegetable tagine **104**, 105
    smoky chickpeas with sundried tomatoes 89
chilla – chickpea and spinach pancakes **30**, 31
chilli
    chilli beef with broccoli 90, **91**
    chilli beef burritos with 'cheese wings' 148, **149**
    crispy chilli oil 50, **51**
    pima crazer – Mauritian chilli sauce 157
Chinese sausage, Mauritian moon fan braised chicken rice **60**, 61
chipotle chicken bowl **36**, 37
chocolate
    air-fryer s'mores **192**, 193
    chocolate icing 200, **201**
    cookie for mama 175, **176**
    miso chocolate cookies **172**, 173
    the ultimate chocolate cake in 15 minutes! 200, **201**
    white chocolate and raspberry tiramisu 180, **181**
cinnamon 19
    cinnamon doughnuts **186**, 187
    cinnamon sugar **186**, 187
coconut (desiccated)
    coconut basbousa 184, **185**
    creamy corn pudding 21
coconut milk
    black bean stew with plantain 64
    Cajun seafood stew 68, **69**
    coconut mango overnight oats **18**, 19
    creamy coconut tomato daal 45
    creamy corn pudding 21
    five-ingredient coconut chicken curry **124**, 125
    lamb meatball red Thai curry **66**, 67
    prawn and plantain curry **102**, 103
    Saturday soup with dumplings 110, **111**
    Thai coconut curry noodle soup 136, **137**
coconut yoghurt
    cinnamon doughnuts **186**, 187
    green biriyani **54**, 55
cod, Cajun seafood stew 68, **69**
coffee, white chocolate and raspberry tiramisu 180, **181**
comfort food 96–125
condensed milk, easy pistachio barfi **196**, 197, **202**
cookies
    cookie for mama 175, **176**
    ghriba – Moroccan cookies 183
    miso chocolate cookies **172**, 173
coriander (fresh) 31, 37–8, 41–2, 45, 49–50, 86, 106, 141
corned beef rougaille 88
cornflour 100, 114, 177
cornmeal, creamy corn pudding 21
cream 89, 109, 117
    creamy garlic chicken pasta **58**, 59
    Swiss roll cake 194, **195**, **202**
    white chocolate and raspberry tiramisu 180, **181**
Creole sauce, prawns in **76**, 77
croissants, pistachio 24, **25**, **32**
cucumber 38, 42, 83, 86
    spicy tuna and cucumber salad 44
curry
    five-ingredient coconut chicken curry **124**, 125
    lamb meatball red Thai curry **66**, 67
    prawn butter masala **108**, 109
    prawn and plantain curry **102**, 103
    speedy masala beans 20
    Thai coconut curry noodle soup 136, **137**

daal
    creamy coconut tomato 45
    see also mung dal
domoda – peanut stew with okra and sweet potato 121
doughnuts, cinnamon **186**, 187
dressings 40, 41–2, **43**, 56, **57**
    spicy peanut 86, **87**
dumplings
    Saturday soup with dumplings 110, **111**
    udon and dumpling ramen 112, **113**

edamame bean 42
egg
    air-fried chicken 100, **101**
    air-fryer cherry pie pockets **176**, 177
    classic Mauritian maspain 174
    coconut basbousa 184, **185**
    cookie for mama 175, **176**
    fluffy yoghurt pancakes **28**, 29, **33**
    funfetti traybake 190, **191**, **202–3**
    ghriba – Moroccan cookies 183
    golden air-fryer muffins 27
    loaded breakfast quiche **16**, 17, **32–3**
    nasi goreng **130**, 131
    pistachio and rose loaf **178**, 179
    roti canai eggs with a mango twist 22, **23**
    savoury cabbage pancakes **94**, 95
    spicy egg bagel 26
    the ultimate chocolate cake in 15 minutes! 200, **201**
equipment 11
everyday heroes 126–48
extras 150–69

filo pastry, crinkle baklava tray **188**, 189
fish
    blackened salmon tacos with mango salsa **118**, 119
    brown stew salmon 138
    Cajun seafood stew 68, **69**
    'marry me' salmon **116**, 117
    salmon teriyaki rice 56, **57**
    spicy tuna and cucumber salad 44
    tuna suugo with baasta 80
five-spice beef noodles **144**, 145
freezing food 10, 211
fritters, spicy sweetcorn **48**, 49
funfetti traybake 190, **191**, **202–3**

garlic
    creamy garlic chicken pasta **58**, 59
    garlic yoghurt **140**, 141
    garlic yoghurt sauce **134**, 135
    garlicky lemon broccoli 156
ghriba – Moroccan cookies 183
gluten-free recipes 204
    air-fried chicken 100, **101**
    black bean stew with plantain 64
    chilla – chickpea and spinach pancakes **30**, 31
    chipotle chicken bowl **36**, 37
    cinnamon doughnuts **186**, 187
    coconut mango overnight oats **18**, 19
    creamy corn pudding 21
    crispy rice salad 42
    domoda – peanut stew with okra and sweet potato 121

green biriyani **54**, 55
harissa roasted pumpkin and chickpeas 46, **47**
prawns in Creole sauce **76**, 77
speedy masala beans 20
sticky mushroom rice 39
gram flour 49
Greek-style yoghurt 27, 142, 154, 184
    fluffy yoghurt pancakes **28**, 29, **33**
    garlic yoghurt **140**, 141
    garlic yoghurt sauce **134**, 135
green bean 165

halloumi and mango shake-up salad **40**, 41
harira, Moroccan 114
harissa roasted pumpkin and chickpeas 46, **47**
honey
    honeyed carrots 160
    miso honey aubergine steaks **146**, 147

icing **178**, 179, 190, **191**, 200, **201**
ingredient sharing 205

jalapeño 37, 44
jam (apricot), ghriba – Moroccan cookies 183
jollof, chicken **72**, 73

kebabs
    air-fryer 122, **123**
    Cevapi – juicy grilled Balkan **84**, 85
    chicken traybake 142, 143
Korean tofu jiggae **92**, 93

lamb
    air-fryer kebabs 122, **123**
    lamb meatball red Thai curry **66**, 67
    Turkish lamb and aubergine traybake 71
    Turkish pizza bread 83
    Turkish-style pasta with garlic yoghurt 141
lemon garlicky broccoli 156
lentil(s)
    creamy coconut tomato daal 45
    Mauritian carrot and red lentil soup 115
    Moroccan harira 114
lettuce 37, 38, 41
lollies, mango lime 182
lunchtimes 34–50

macaroni cheese, cheesy microwave mac magic 132, **133**
mangetout 38
mango 38, 42
    coconut mango overnight oats **18**, 19
    mango and halloumi shake-up salad **40**, 41
    mango lime lollies 182

mango salsa **118**, 119
roti canai eggs with a mango twist 22, **23**
maple syrup 19, 147
marshmallow, air-fryer s'mores **192**, 193
masala
    prawn butter masala **108**, 109
    speedy masala beans 20
mascarpone
    pistachio croissants 24, **25**, **32**
    white chocolate and raspberry tiramisu 180, **181**
maspain, classic Mauritian 174
meal plans 206–7
meatballs, lamb meatball red Thai curry **66**, 67
microwave recipes 204
    cheesy microwave mac magic 132, **133**
    creamy coconut tomato daal 45
    microwave shortbread **198**, 199
    speedy masala beans 20
    spicy egg bagel 26
mint 31, 38, 41
miso
    miso chocolate cookies **172**, 173
    miso honey aubergine steaks **146**, 147
Moroccan harira 114
Moroccan vegetable tagine **104**, 105
Moulouktani chicken, Mauritian 120
mozzarella cheese
    chilli beef burritos with 'cheese wings' 148, **149**
    paratha chilli-cheese rolls **82**, 91
    pull-apart pizza rolls **98**, 99
    quick cheesy naan 154, **155**
muffins, golden air-fryer 27
mung dal, Mauritian Moulouktani chicken 120
mushroom 61
    sticky mushroom rice 39
mussel(s), Cajun seafood stew 68, **69**

naan, quick cheesy 154, **155**
nasi goreng **130**, 131
noodles
    five-spice beef noodles **144**, 145
    Mauritian noodles 62, **63**
    rainbow noodles 86, **87**
    Thai coconut curry noodle soup 136, **137**
    udon and dumpling ramen 112, **113**

oat(s), coconut mango overnight **18**, 19
okra, *domoda* – peanut stew with okra and sweet potato 121
onion and sumac salad 142, **143**
orange blossom water 183
organisational skills 10

pak choi 62, 112, 136
pancakes
    chilla – chickpea and spinach **30**, 31
    fluffy yoghurt **28**, 29, **33**
    savoury cabbage **94**, 95
paratha chilli-cheese rolls **82**, 91
Parmesan cheese, creamy garlic chicken pasta **58**, 59
passata, prawn butter masala **108**, 109
pasta
    cheesy microwave mac magic 132, **133**
    creamy garlic chicken pasta **58**, 59
    Moroccan harira 114
    spaghetti Bolognese **128**, 129
    tuna suugo with baasta 80
    Turkish-style pasta with garlic yoghurt **140**, 141
peanut
    crispy rice salad 42
    rainbow noodles 86, **87**
peanut butter
    domoda – peanut stew with okra and sweet potato 121
    satay chicken drumsticks 139
    spicy peanut dressing 86, **87**
pea(s) 17, 55
pepper 41, 56, 64, 67, 68, 71, 73, 86, 103, 106, 138
pepperoni, pull-apart pizza rolls **98**, 99
peri peri traybake chicken 106, **107**
pickles, zasar legim – spicy Mauritian pickled **164**, 165
pie pockets, air-fryer cherry **176**, 177
pilaf, chicken bulgur 65
pima crazer – Mauritian chilli sauce 157
pineapple fried rice with cashews 78, **79**
pistachio
    easy pistachio barfi **196**, 197, **202**
    pistachio croissants 24, **25**, **32**
    pistachio and rose loaf **178**, 179
pizza
    pull-apart pizza rolls **98**, 99
    Turkish pizza bread 83
plantain
    black bean stew with plantain 64
    plantains 161
    prawn and plantain curry **102**, 103
potato 71, 169
    the best roast potatoes **158**, 159
    Moroccan vegetable tagine **104**, 105
prawn
    Cajun seafood stew 68, **69**
    prawn butter masala **108**, 109
    prawn and plantain curry **102**, 103
    prawns in Creole sauce **76**, 77
    Thai coconut curry noodle soup 136, **137**
puff pastry, air-fryer cherry pie pockets **176**, 177
pumpkin, harissa roasted pumpkin and chickpeas 46, **47**

quiche, loaded breakfast **16**, 17, **32–3**
quick meals 74–95

rainbow noodles 86, **87**
ramen, udon and dumpling 112, **113**
raspberry
    mango lime lollies 182
    pistachio croissants 24, **25**, **32**
    white chocolate and raspberry tiramisu 180, **181**
    Red Leicester cheese, chilli beef burritos with 'cheese wings' 148, **149**
    red wine, spaghetti Bolognese **128**, 129
    reheating food 10, 211
rice
    chicken jollof **72**, 73
    chicken peri peri traybake 106, **107**
    crispy rice salad 42
    everyday rice 166
    golden spiced rice 169
    green biriyani **54**, 55
    Mauritian moon fan braised chicken rice **60**, 61
    nasi goreng **130**, 131
    pineapple fried rice with cashews 78, **79**
    red rice 167
    salmon teriyaki rice 56, **57**
    sticky mushroom rice 39
    sushi rice waffle, tomatoes and a crispy chilli oil 50, **51**
flour 49, 95
rice paper wrappers, fresh and crunchy summer rolls 38
rose water
    pistachio and rose loaf **178**, 179
    syrup **184**, 185
roti canai eggs with a mango twist 22, 23
rotis, veggie **152**, 153
rougaille, corned beef 88

salads
    crispy rice 42
    mango and halloumi shake-up **40**, 41
    onion and sumac 142, **143**
    spicy tuna and cucumber 44
salmon
    blackened salmon tacos with mango salsa **118**, 119
    brown stew salmon 138
    'marry me' salmon **116**, 117
    salmon teriyaki rice 56, **57**
salsa
    mango **118**, 119
    tomato and coriander 141
satay chicken drumsticks 139
Saturday soup with dumplings 110, **111**

sauces 12
    for chilli beef with broccoli 90, **91**
    Creole sauce **76**, 77
    for five-spice beef noodles **144**, 145
    garlic yoghurt sauce **134**, 135
    'marry me' sauce **116**, 117
    for Mauritian noodles 62, **63**
    pima crazer – Mauritian chilli sauce 157
seafood stew, Cajun 68, **69**
semolina 184
shawarma, chicken **134**, 135
shortbread, microwave **198**, 199
s'mores, air-fryer **192**, 193
soup
    Mauritian carrot and red lentil soup 115
    Moroccan harira 114
    Saturday soup with dumplings 110, **111**
    Thai coconut curry noodle soup 136, **137**
soured cream 37
spaghetti Bolognese **128**, 129
spices 12, 208–9
spinach and chickpea pancakes **30**, 31
stew
    black bean stew with plantain 64
    brown stew salmon 138
    Cajun seafood stew 68, **69**
    domoda – peanut stew with okra and sweet potato 121
    see also tagine
sugar
    cinnamon sugar **186**, 187
    sugar syrup **188**, 189
sumac and onion salad 142, **143**
summer rolls, fresh and crunchy 38
sushi rice waffle, tomatoes and a crispy chilli oil 50, **51**
suugo, tuna suugo with baasta 80
sweet fixes 170–200
sweet potato 68
    domoda – peanut stew with okra and sweet potato 121
sweetcorn 17, 62, 68, 110
    spicy sweetcorn fritters **48**, 49
    sweetcorn ribs 162, **163**
Swiss roll cake 194, **195**, **202**
syrup 184, **185**
    sugar syrup **188**, 189

tacos, blackened salmon tacos with mango salsa **118**, 119
tagine, Moroccan vegetable **104**, 105
Tenderstem broccoli, garlicky lemon 156
Thai coconut curry noodle soup 136, 137
tiramisu, white chocolate and raspberry 180, 181

tofu
- Korean tofu jiggae 92, 93
- Thai coconut curry noodle soup 136, **137**

tomato
- chicken jollof **72**, 73
- corned beef rougaille 88
- creamy coconut tomato daal 45
- loaded breakfast quiche **16**, 17, **32–3**
- mango and halloumi shake-up salad **40**, 41
- 'marry me' sauce **116**, 117
- Mauritian carrot and red lentil soup 115
- prawns in Creole sauce **76**, 77
- red rice 167
- roti canai eggs with a mango twist 22, **23**
- smoky chickpeas with sundried tomatoes 89
- spaghetti Bolognese **128**, 129
- sushi rice waffle, tomatoes and a crispy chilli oil 50, **51**
- tomato and coriander salsa 141
- tuna suugo with baasta 80
- Turkish pizza bread 83
- *see also* passata

tortillas
- chilli beef burritos with 'cheese wings' 148, **149**
- loaded breakfast quiche **16**, 17, **32–3**

tuna
- spicy tuna and cucumber salad 44
- tuna suugo with baasta 80

Turkish lamb and aubergine traybake 71
Turkish pizza bread 83
Turkish-style pasta with garlic yoghurt **140**, 141

udon and dumpling ramen 112, **113**

vanilla
- classic Mauritian maspain 174
- coconut basbousa 184, **185**
- cookie for mama 175, **176**
- creamy corn pudding 21
- funfetti traybake 190, **191**, **202–3**
- the ultimate chocolate cake in 15 minutes! 200, **201**
- white chocolate and raspberry tiramisu 180, **181**

vegan/vegetarian recipes 204
- chilla – chickpea and spinach pancakes **30**, 31
- coconut mango overnight oats **18**, 19
- creamy coconut tomato daal 45
- crispy rice salad 42
- fluffy yoghurt pancakes **28**, 29, **33**
- fresh and crunchy summer rolls 38
- funfetti traybake 190, **191**, **202–3**
- ghriba – Moroccan cookies 183
- harissa roasted pumpkin and chickpeas 46, **47**
- pistachio and rose loaf **178**, 179
- speedy masala beans 20

veggie rotis **152**, 153
vermicelli pasta, Moroccan harira 114

waffles, sushi rice waffle, tomatoes and a crispy chilli oil 50, **51**
walnut, crinkle baklava tray **188**, 189
white chocolate and raspberry tiramisu 180, **181**

yoghurt *see* coconut yoghurt; Greek-style yoghurt

zasar legim – spicy Mauritian pickled **164**, 165

Note: page numbers in **bold** refer to recipe illustrations.

Conversion Guides

WEIGHTS

Metric	Imperial
15g	½ oz
25g	1 oz
40g	1½ oz
50g	2 oz
75g	3 oz
100g	4 oz
150g	5 oz
175g	6 oz
200g	7 oz
225g	8 oz
250g	9 oz
275g	10 oz
350g	12 oz
375g	13 oz
400g	14 oz
425g	15 oz
450g	1 lb
550g	1¼ lb
675g	1½ lb
900g	2 lb
1.5kg	3 lb
1.75kg	4 lb
2.25kg	5 lb

VOLUME

Metric	Imperial
25ml	1 fl oz
50ml	2 fl oz
85ml	3 fl oz
150ml	5 fl oz (¼ pint)
300ml	10 fl oz (½ pint)
450ml	15 fl oz (¾ pint)
600ml	1 pint
700ml	1¼ pints
900ml	1½ pints
1 litre	1¾ pints
1.2 litres	2 pints
1.25 litres	2¼ pints
1.5 litres	2½ pints
1.6 litres	2¾ pints
1.75 litres	3 pints
1.8 litres	3¼ pints
2 litres	3½ pints
2.1 litres	3¾ pints
2.25 litres	4 pints
2.75 litres	5 pints
3.4 litres	6 pints
3.9 litres	7 pints
5 litres	8 pints (1 gal)

MEASUREMENTS

Metric	Imperial
0.5cm	¼ inch
1cm	½ inch
2.5cm	1 inch
5cm	2 inches
7.5cm	3 inches
10cm	4 inches

Metric	Imperial
15cm	6 inches
18cm	7 inches
20cm	8 inches
23cm	9 inches
25cm	10 inches
30cm	12 inches

OVEN TEMPERATURES

°C	Fan °C	°F	Gas Mark
140°C	120°C	275°F	Gas Mark 1
150°C	130°C	300°F	Gas Mark 2
160°C	140°C	325°F	Gas Mark 3
180°C	160°C	350°F	Gas Mark 4
190°C	170°C	375°F	Gas Mark 5
200°C	180°C	400°F	Gas Mark 6
220°C	200°C	425°F	Gas Mark 7
230°C	210°C	450°F	Gas Mark 8
240°C	220°C	475°F	Gas Mark 9

Acknowledgements

This book would not exist without the unwavering support and love of my daughter Niyyah, who is the inspiration behind everything I do. You remind me every day why I cook with love.

To my family, thank you for feeding my dreams long before I knew where they would take me. Your traditions, laughter, open criticism (Mauritian households you get what I mean) and food have shaped me in every way.

To my friends, the ones who drop by for dinner, bring stories and leave with leftovers, thank you for being my cheerleaders and happy recipe testers.

To the wonderful team at Ebury who have been with me for the long run. A heartfelt thank you, especially to Ru, Liv and Emille, who have gone the extra mile to support me and get me to the finishing line. And to Emily, my brilliant literary agent, for taking a chance on me and putting me back out in the world.

To my readers and longstanding supporters, thank you for choosing this book. I hope it becomes your companion in the kitchen and makes life just that little bit easier.

About the Author

Shelina Permalloo is a British-Mauritian chef, author and entrepreneur. A passionate advocate of flavour-packed, accessible cooking, she rose to fame after winning BBC's *MasterChef* and has since built a career sharing vibrant, honest food inspired by her heritage and motherhood.

As a single mum and busy entrepreneur and professional chef for over a decade, Shelina understands the real-life pressures of feeding a family while juggling a million other roles. This book is a tribute to that everyday hustle, filled with recipes that are quick, comforting and full of life. Her cooking reflects her roots – warm, colourful and unapologetically bold.

EBURY PRESS

UK | USA | Canada | Ireland | Australia
India | New Zealand | South Africa

Ebury Press is part of the Penguin Random House group of companies whose addresses can be found at global.penguinrandomhouse.com

Penguin Random House UK
One Embassy Gardens, 8 Viaduct Gardens, London SW11 7BW

penguin.co.uk

First published by Ebury Press in 2026

1

Copyright © Shelina Permalloo 2026
Photography © Danielle Wood 2026

The moral right of the author has been asserted.

Penguin Random House values and supports copyright. Copyright fuels creativity, encourages diverse voices, promotes freedom of expression and supports a vibrant culture. Thank you for purchasing an authorised edition of this book and for respecting intellectual property laws by not reproducing, scanning or distributing any part of it by any means without permission. You are supporting authors and enabling Penguin Random House to continue to publish books for everyone. No part of this book may be used or reproduced in any manner for the purpose of training artificial intelligence technologies or systems. In accordance with Article 4(3) of the DSM Directive 2019/790, Penguin Random House expressly reserves this work from the text and data mining exception.

Editorial Director: Ru Merritt
Senior Editor: Liv Nightingall
Editorial Assistant: Emille Bwale
Production: Lucy Harrison
Designer: George Saad
Photographer: Danielle Wood
Food Stylist: Lou Kenney
Food Stylist Assistant: Hattie Baker
Prop Stylist: Max Robinson

Colour origination by Altaimage Ltd
Printed and bound in China by C&C Offset Printing Co., Ltd

The authorised representative in the EEA is Penguin Random House Ireland, Morrison Chambers, 32 Nassau Street, Dublin D02 YH68.

A CIP catalogue record for this book is available from the British Library

ISBN 9781529966435

Penguin Random House is committed to a sustainable future for our business, our readers and our planet. This book is made from Forest Stewardship Council® certified paper.